Oracle Grid & Real Application Clusters
Oracle Grid Computing with RAC

Steve Karam
Bryan Jones

RAMPANT
TECHPRESS

To Janelle, Annie, Jenson and Elisabeth, and to my Parents. I am grateful for all of you. Thanks for everything.

Bryan Jones

Oracle Grid & Real Application Clusters
Oracle Grid Computing with RAC

By Steve Karam and Bryan Jones

Copyright © 2010 by Rampant TechPress. All rights reserved.
Printed in the United States of America.
Published in Kittrell, North Carolina, USA.

Oracle In-focus Series: Book #32

Series Editor: Donald K. Burleson

Production Manager: Robin Rademacher

Editor: Valerre Aquitaine

Production Editor: Robin Rademacher

Cover Design: Janet Burleson

Printing History: July, 2010 for First Edition, March 2014 Softcover Edition

Oracle, Oracle7, Oracle8, Oracle8i, Oracle9i, Oracle10g, Oracle11g and Oracle12c are trademarks of Oracle Corporation.

Many of the designations used by computer vendors to distinguish their products are claimed as Trademarks. All names known by Rampant TechPress to be trademark names appear in this text as initial caps.

Flame Warriors illustrations are copyright © by Mike Reed Illustrations Inc.

The information provided by the authors of this work is believed to be accurate and reliable. However, because of the possibility of human error by our authors and staff, Rampant TechPress cannot guarantee the accuracy or completeness of any information included in this work and is not responsible for any errors, omissions, or inaccurate results obtained from the use of information or scripts in this work.

ISBN 10: 0-9916386-2-X
ISBN 13: 978-0-9916386-2-8

Library of Congress Control Number: 2009926794

Table of Contents

Using the Online Code Depot

Purchase of this book provides complete access to the online code depot that contains sample code scripts. Any code depot scripts in this book are located at the following URL in zip format and ready to load and use:

rampant.cc/11g_Grid_RAC.htm

If technical assistance is needed with downloading or accessing the scripts, please contact Rampant TechPress at rtp@rampant.cc.

Conventions Used in this Book

It is critical for any technical publication to follow rigorous standards and employ consistent punctuation conventions to make the text easy to read. However, this is not an easy task. Within database terminology, there are many types of notation that can confuse a reader. For example, some Oracle utilities such as STATSPACK and TKPROF are always spelled in CAPITAL letters, while Oracle parameters and procedures have varying naming conventions in the database documentation. It is also important to remember that many database commands are case sensitive, and are always left in their original executable form, and never altered with italics or capitalization. Hence, all Rampant TechPress books follow these conventions:

Parameters – Database parameters will be *lowercase italics*. The exception is parameter arguments that are commonly capitalized (KEEP pool, TKPROF), which will be ALL CAPS.

Variables – Procedural language (e.g. PL/SQL) program variables and arguments will also remain in *lowercase italics* (i.e. *dbms_job*).

Tables & dictionary objects – Data dictionary objects are referenced in lowercase italics (*dba_indexes*, *v$sql*), ncluding *v$* and *x$* views (*x$kcbcbh*, *v$parameter*) and dictionary views (*dba_tables*, *user_indexes*).

SQL – All SQL is formatted for easy use in the code depot and displayed in lowercase. Main SQL terms (select, from, where, group by, order by, having) will appear on a separate line.

Programs & Products – All products and programs that are known to the author are capitalized according to the vendor specifications (CentOS, VMware, Oracle, etc). All names known by Rampant TechPress to be trademark names appear in this text as initial caps. References to UNIX are always made in uppercase.

Acknowledgements

This type of highly technical reference book requires the dedicated efforts of many people. Even though we are the authors, our work ends when we deliver the content. After each chapter is delivered, several Oracle DBAs carefully review and correct the technical content. After the technical review, experienced copy editors polish the grammar and syntax.

The finished work is then reviewed as page proofs and turned over to the production manager, who arranges the creation of the online code depot and manages the cover art, printing distribution, and warehousing.

In short, the authors play a small role in the development of this book, and we need to thank and acknowledge everyone who helped bring this book to fruition:

Robin Rademacher, for the production management, including the coordination of the cover art, page proofing, printing, and distribution.

Valerre Aquitaine, for help in the production of the page proofs.

Janet Burleson, for exceptional cover design and graphics.

John Lavender, for assistance with the web site, and for creating the code depot and the online shopping cart for this book.

Special thanks to Mike Ault and Madhu Tumma for use of material from "Oracle 10g Grid and Real Application Clusters."

With our sincerest thanks,

Steve Karam & Bryan Jones

Intro to RAC and Grid Computing

"Press 1 for automatic grid provisioning, press 2 for rolling upgrades, or press 3 for hot patching."

What is Grid Computing?

According to DEGREE (www.eu-degree.eu), grid computing "provides the ability to perform higher throughput computing by taking advantage of many networked computers to model a virtual computer architecture that is able to distribute process execution across a parallel infrastructure." Grids allow a computational power far exceeding what is possible on one server.

Grid computing is a type of distributed computing. In general, a distributed computing program is divided into many parts to run on multiple servers connected via a network. Grid computing coordinates the sharing of CPU, application, data, storage and network resources. Grid computing is the pool of computers actively glued into a virtual computing architecture by the other related components such as

---

middleware software, interconnects, networking devices, and storage units.

Oracle's implementation of grid architecture is one of the most widely used commercial grid capable products. The Open Grid Forum (OGF) is the current international standards body for grid computing. OGF's members consist of 400 organizations in over 50 countries. OGF works to increase the adoption of grid computing and create standards that facilitate interoperability.

Where is the IT World on Grid Computing?

In many ways, grid computing is a solution without any problems to solve. The pioneers of grid computing are ready to solve the hardest problems that any industry is willing to throw at them. The task at hand is to find more problems that need to be solved.

Main industries embracing grid computing:

- aerospace
- automotive
- insurance
- investment banking
- finance
- gaming
- government
- media
- oil / gas / earth science
- online advertising
- semiconductor
- telecommunication
- pharmaceuticals

What is Oracle's Direction?

Grid computing software is much more complex to create than typical software. With each release of Oracle RAC, true grid capabilities are evolving to be more feature-rich. Database market share is ultra-competitive. As Oracle successfully tackles various grid computing complexities and their competitors lag years and decades behind, Oracle will logically charge ahead to make their grid computing capabilities more feature-complete. One challenge for Oracle and other grid software designers is to make grid computing simpler to use and implement.

Oracle is one of the 400 organizational members of the Open Grid Forum. At the time of this writing, Toshihiro Suzuki is the Senior Director of Standards Strategy and Architecture for Oracle Corporation Japan. Toshihiro is part of the OGF Operational Leadership team. He was chairperson of the OGF ancestor organization, the Enterprise Grid Alliance (EGA).

One reason why this newfound love for grid computing has evolved is because of the appeal of power. The computational power that grid computing offers makes the Intel and AMD CPU Gigahertz race somewhat irrelevant. Instead of waiting around for CPU power to be 1,000 times faster than it is today, an engineer can simply take advantage of the massive computational power that grid computing provides.

For academic researchers, grid computing offers low cost CPU power that is much less expensive and freely available. Today, Sun Microsystems offers "Sun Utility Computing." After a simple pre-approval process, anyone can gain access to thousands of CPUs at once. If one has ever wondered what the highest prime number a grid system can find in less than 5 minutes is, then Sun Utility Computing is the chance to find out!

This quote from Sun Microsystems states, "For each job the user submits and runs, the user's Sun Grid CPU usage is aggregated and then rounded up to the nearest whole hour. For example, if your job used 1000 CPUs for one minute, it would be aggregated as 1000 CPU minutes or 16.67 CPU hours. The software rounds this up to 17 hours and the job would be billed as US $17."

Grid Types

This is not a complete list, but a starting point to learn about grid types. The grid types listed below are not mutually exclusive. Many grid implementations have attributes belonging to multiple grid types.

- Clusters
- Data Grid
- Compute Grid
- Enterprise Grid
- Department Grid
- Open Grid
- Partner Grid
- Scavenging Grid

Clusters

Dr. Robert Cohen, in his paper "Cluster and Grid Computing in Japan: Today and in 2010" explains, "Clusters are a first step in the use of grids." Clusters are multiple servers, usually combined via some type of network protocol to provide high availability or load balancing.

Data Grid

A data grid is the storage piece of a grid. A data grid is responsible for housing and providing access to data. Users do not need to be concerned with the location of the data or how wide the data is distributed. The data set sizes used in grid computing are sometimes revolutionarily large. Data grid performance depends on the network connection speed, because a grid is highly network-dependent.

Compute Grid

A compute grid is created for computational intensive batch applications. Batch jobs times vary and can be measured in microseconds or years. Sun Microsystems claims that the Sun Grid is "the world's first and only true compute utility."

Enterprise Grid

According to the OGF, "An enterprise grid is a collection of interconnected (networked) grid components under the control of a grid management entity (GME). An enterprise grid is typically managed by a single enterprise - i.e. a business entity is responsible for managing the assignment of resources to services in order to meet its business goals. The resources and services may or may not be owned by the business; for example, in the case of managed services or a service provider/outsourcer. An enterprise grid may be confined to a single data center or it may extend across several."

Department Grid

A department grid is an enterprise grid on a smaller scale.

Open Grid

According to Grid Wise Tech, "Open grids provide controlled access to resources, services and applications for the public."

Partner Grid

According to Grid Wise Tech, "Partner grids enable collaboration and resource sharing between business partners within a dynamic security framework."

Scavenging Grid

A scavenging grid is most commonly used with large numbers of desktop machines. Machines are scavenged for available CPU cycles and other resources. Owners of the desktop machines are usually given control over when their resources are available to participate in the grid.

Grids and Clusters

The key distinction between clusters and grids lies mainly in the way the resources are managed. In the case of clusters, a centralized resource manager performs the resource allocation, and all nodes cooperatively work together as a single unified resource running on the same operating system and hardware architecture. The result of such aggregation is to present a single system image (SSI). Clusters are generally built for a specific purpose; for instance, to host a parallel database server or for hosting an application server. In the case of grids, each node has its own resource manager and does not aim for providing a single system view. They, in turn, provide a pool of resources for a variety of users and applications.

Grids can span across single or multiple organizations and data centers. Grids encompass a bigger framework and provide wider and loosely coupled aggregation of servers and other related resources.

Grid architecture employs specialized scheduling software GME (Grid Management Entity) that identifies available resources and allocates tasks for processing accordingly. Requests for resources are processed wherever it is most efficient or wherever a specific function resides. Computers or nodes located in the grid are able to act independently without centralized control, handling requests as they are made and scheduling others. If one set of resources is not available, they will simply use another.

Introduction to Cluster Technology

A cluster consists of servers linked via a network interconnect that present a single system image (SSI) to users and applications. Clusters are used to provide HA (high availability) and load balancing. RAC (Real Application Cluster) is a clustering solution for Oracle databases. The software glue that holds the Oracle 11g RAC together is called Oracle Clusterware. Clusterware coordinates database operations between servers so that the SSI is maintained.

Clusterware is required on all Oracle 11g RAC implementations, regardless of the operating system or additional cluster software being used. Any additional third party cluster software must be certified for RAC.

Oracle Clusterware

Oracle Clusterware manages node membership, group services, global resource management, and high availability functions. Clusterware is a prerequisite to the Oracle RAC installation. A RAC database is managed by clusterware. Other Oracle processes that are managed by clusterware are the VIP, Global Services Daemon (GSD), the Oracle Notification Services (ONS), and the listeners. These processes are started automatically by clusterware and restarted when failures occur. Clusterware is installed from one node (server), but the clusterware daemons are installed and run on all cluster nodes.

Clusterware essentially manages all cluster-aware processes. These processes are called CRS resources in 11g. The resource settings are stored in the Oracle Cluster Registry (OCR). The main clusterware resources are listed here.

- Database
- Instances
- Services
- Listeners
- VIP address

Database to Instance One-to-Many Relationship

Prior to Oracle RAC, the terms Oracle instance and Oracle database were often used interchangeably. In the RAC world, the distinction is much clearer, because the instance and database no longer have a one-to-one relationship. Oracle RAC systems have a one-to-many relationship between the database and the instances. Each instance runs on a separate server. Oracle RAC instances have their own initialization parameter file, redo thread, redo log files and undo tablespace.

An Oracle RAC database consists of 2+ database instances. Each instance has its own memory structures and background processes similar to a non-RAC instance. Oracle RAC instances also have additional memory structures and background processes.

According to Oracle's documentation, an Oracle 11g RAC database can have as many as one hundred instances. Implementing a production of a one-hundred-instance RAC system as one's first RAC experience should only be done with one's resume prominently posted on Monster and HotJobs.com. In other words, one's first RAC implementation should not be a bite that is more than one can chew.

Maximum Availability

For maximum availability, Oracle Data Guard with Oracle RAC can provide HA even when the local data center is completely down. The key features of Oracle RAC are high availability and scalability. Multiple instances on multiple servers ensure that a single server is not a single point of failure.

Shared Cluster Architecture

Unlike the 'shared nothing' Google search platform, Oracle RAC is a shared everything database. The following items are shared by all RAC instances.

- data files
- control files
- SPFILEs
- redo log files (shared during recovery)

- interconnect

Since Oracle RAC is a shared everything system, the data files, control files, SPFILEs and redo log files must reside on cluster aware shared storage.

Storage Options

The shared storage options for Oracle 11g RAC are ASM, OCFS for Windows, OCFS2 for Linux, NFS (now with Direct NFS in 11g), certified third-party cluster-aware volume manager, certified network file system, and raw devices. Oracle requires that RAC implementations using Network Attached Storage (NAS) use their own private network, which is separate from the interconnect.

Metalink Note 578455.1 indicates Oracle's support of raw devices is going away in Oracle 12g.

Virtual IP Address

Unlike a single instance database, an Oracle RAC instance can be connected to a client through the server's IP address and through VIP addresses. The VIP address or corresponding virtual host name is the logical way to connect to the RAC database, because of the built-in failover ability.

🖧 **Code Depot Username = reader, Password = 11grac**

Interconnect

The interconnect is a critical component of the Oracle RAC architecture.

From Oracle: "The interconnect network is a private network that connects all of the servers in the cluster. The interconnect network uses a switch (or multiple switches) that only the nodes in the cluster can access. Configure User Datagram Protocol (UDP) on a Gigabit you can configure Oracle Clusterware to use either the UDP or Reliable Data

Socket (RDS) protocols. Windows clusters use the TCP protocol. Crossover cables are not supported for use with Oracle Clusterware interconnects."

Using 10 Gigabit Ethernet as the interconnect is not mentioned above by Oracle, but is a good choice because it can move 1,250 MB/s versus Gigabit Ethernet's 125 MB/s.

Cache Fusion

Cache Fusion is a core part of Oracle RAC. The System Global Area (SGA) consists of multiple components, one of which is the buffer cache. In RAC, cache fusion combines the buffer cache, allowing the buffer cache size to be much larger. Cache fusion traffic and other inter-instance communication takes place over the RAC interconnect private network.

A data block initially resides on disk. As queries are run, data blocks are copied from disk to the requesting instance's buffer cache. If another instance needs any of the data blocks that are now in the first instance's buffer cache, the second instance will obtain the blocks from the first instance, preventing a more expensive trip to disk. The Global Cache Service (GCS) and the Global Enqueue Service (GES) processes keep track of the status of each cached block using a memory resident data structure called the Global Resource Directory (GRD).

There are a number of RAC specific processes which will be explained in more detail in other chapters. The processes are ACMS, GTX0-j, LMON, LMD, LMS, LCK0, RMSn and RSMN.

High Performance, Availability and Computing

Highly available and scalable computer systems and applications are an essential part of today's business environment. This is achieved by cluster technology and fault tolerant systems. The server clustering

---

technology that supports both high performance computing and high availability has been widely used for over a decade.

Research institutions have always been in the forefront in using high performance computers. Analysis of large datasets and complex algorithms in academic research is common.

The Internet, with its potential to connect virtually every computer in the world, has made database technology more crucial than ever. With increasing numbers of users connecting concurrently to databases to query and update data, high performing servers are essential. Uneven workload patterns and long running complex data warehousing applications require high performing database technology. Database software must be able to cope with increased demands and complexity.

To optimize the data storage and retrieval, parallel execution or parallel processing is one of the most effective methods. Parallel execution focuses on achieving faster response times and better utilization of multiple CPU resources on the database server. Many database management systems, including Oracle, leverage the availability of faster and multi-CPU computers to process and retrieve data by utilizing parallel processing methodology.

Parallel Processing

Parallel execution or processing involves dividing a task into several smaller tasks and working on each of those smaller tasks in parallel. In a parallel processing system, multiple processes may reside on a single computer or they may be spread across separate computers or nodes as in a cluster.

In clustered architecture, two or more nodes, or servers, are interconnected and share common storage resources. Each node has its own set of processors. A cluster is usually an aggregation of multiple SMP nodes. Scalability is better achieved in a cluster on a modular basis. As the need arises, additional servers can be added to a cluster.

Scalability

Scalability is the ability to maintain higher performance levels as the workload increases by incrementally adding more system capacity in terms of more processors and memory. On a single processor system, it becomes difficult to achieve scalability beyond a certain point. Parallelization, by using multi-processor servers, provides better scalability than single processor systems.

Scalability can be understood from two different perspectives: a speed-up of tasks within the system and an increase in concurrency in the system, sometimes referred to as scale-up.

There are two ways to achieve speed-up of tasks:

- Increasing the execution capacity of the existing hardware components of a server through multiple CPUs

- Breaking the job into multiple sub-tasks and assigning these components to multiple processors to execute them concurrently

Parallel Databases

Modern relational database systems are typically architected with parallel capable software that is well suited to take advantage of the parallel architecture of SMP systems. The Oracle database system is a multi-process application in UNIX systems and is a multi-threaded application under the Windows architecture.

Databases have a component called the query optimizer, which selects a sequence of inputs, joins, and scans to produce the desired output table or data set. The query optimizer is aware of the underlying hardware architecture to utilize the suitable path for invoking parallel execution. Thus, from the database point-of-view, parallel execution is useful for all types of operations that access significant amounts of data.

Generally, parallel execution improves performance for:

- queries

- creation of large indexes

- bulk inserts, updates, and deletes

- aggregations and copying

Parallel processing involves the use of multiple processors to reduce the time needed to complete a given task. Instead of one processor executing an entire task, several processors work on separate tasks which are subordinate to the main task. There are several architectural approaches for multiple processor systems. They are:

- Symmetric Multi-Processors (SMP)

- Clustered Systems

- NUMA (or DSM - Distributed Share Model) servers

- MPP (Massively Parallel Processing)

Types of Parallelism

There are two types of parallelism. They are inter-query parallelism and intra-query parallelism.

- **Inter-Query Parallelism** - Individual transactions are independent, and no transaction requires the output of another transaction to complete. Many CPUs can be kept busy by assigning each task or query to a separate CPU. This type of parallelism, where many separate independent queries are active at the same time, is called inter-query parallelism. In an OLTP environment, each query is fairly small, small enough to complete on a single process utilizing a single CPU.

- **Intra-Query Parallelism** - To speed up execution of a large, complex query, it must first be decomposed into smaller problems, and these smaller problems execute concurrently (in parallel) by assigning each sub-problem concurrently to its CPUs. This is called intra-query parallelism. Decision support systems (DSS) need this kind of facility. Data warehousing applications often deal with huge data sets, involving data capture, analysis and summaries, so these operations also require this capability.

Highly Available Databases

The Need for Highly Available Data

Unplanned downtime and planned downtime are costly in terms of lost revenue and time. Planned downtime in one time zone has a direct impact on the business hours of another time zone.

It is important to understand certain key terms and concepts before examining HA systems and databases.

Failure

Failure is defined as a departure from expected behavior on an individual computer system. Software, hardware, operator and procedural errors, along with environmental factors, can each cause a system failure.

Availability

Availability is a measure of the amount of time a system or component performs its specified function. Availability is related to, but differs from, reliability. Reliability measures how frequently the system fails; availability measures the percentage of time the system is in its operational state.

To calculate availability, both the Mean Time Between Failures (MTBF) and the Mean Time To Recovery (MTTR) need to be known. The MTTR is a measure of how long, on average, it takes to restore the system to its operational state after a failure. If both the MTBF and the MTTR are known, availability can be calculated using the following formula:

```
Availability = MTBF / (MTBF + MTTR)
```

For example, if the data center fails roughly every six months (MTBF = six months) and it takes 20 minutes, on average, to return the data center to its operational state (MTTR = 20 minutes), then the data center availability is:

```
Availability = 6 months / (6 months + 20 minutes) = 99.992 percent.
```

Therefore, there are two ways to improve the availability of the system: increase MTBF or reduce MTTR. Having realized that system failures do occur or are unavoidable, system and database administrators need to focus on designing a reliable system with redundant components, as well as setting up reliable recovery methodology for when system failures happen.

Reliability

Reliability is the starting point for building increasingly available systems since a measure of system reliability is how long it has been up and/or how long it typically stays up between failures. The nature of the failure is not important — any failure affects the system's overall availability. As presented in the previous section, MTBF is often considered an important metric with respect to measuring system reliability.

There are two primary means of achieving greater reliability:

- Building high MTBF components into the system
- Adding MTBF components in redundant (N+1) configurations

Serviceability

Serviceability defines the time it takes to isolate and repair a fault or, more succinctly, the time it takes to restore a system to service following a failure. Mean Time To Recovery, or MTTR, is considered an important metric when discussing the serviceability of a system or some component of the system. MTTR, however, is a unit of time and does not factor into the cost of service.

Fault-Tolerant Systems

Another important distinction that needs to be made is between a high availability (HA) system and a fault tolerant (FT) system. Fault tolerant systems offer a higher level of resilience and recovery. They use a high degree of hardware redundancy and specialized software to provide near-instantaneous recovery from any single hardware or software unit failure.

Database Availability

When referring to the availability of databases, the total environment and infrastructure in which a typical database is located needs to be examined. The database application has its own availability features that are unique from the system availability point of view.

There are three situations that need to be considered:

- database server availability
- network availability
- disk storage availability and connectivity

Another important issue relevant for the database is the need to maintain the database consistency. Unlike application servers or other application instances, multiple database instances or copies of databases cannot exist. As the database contents change in real-time, multiple copies cannot be maintained in a timely manner.

Benefits of Real Application Clusters (RAC)

The benefits of Real Application Clusters:

- Ability to spread CPU load across multiple servers
- Continuous Availability / High Availability (HA)
  - Protection from single instance failures
  - Protection from single server failures

- RAC can take advantage of larger SGA sizes than can be accommodated by a single instance commodity server
- Scalability

There are cases where RAC may not be an appropriate option:

- If RAC is being used as a cost savings solution, be sure to analyze both hardware and software costs
- Do not expect RAC to scale if the application will not scale on SMP
- Be realistic about the latency difference between local only memory-cache instance communication and inter-node network based multi-instance Cache Fusion communication

RAC is not always the best option

Solutions such as RAC are not always the best option. If high performance is the only requirement and the single server can consistently deliver the necessary power needed, then a single instance server may be the best choice. If High Availability (HA) is the only requirement, and less complex solutions such as Data Guard are adequate, then Data Guard without RAC might be the best choice.

RAC Evolution

Evolution from OPS

The biggest performance robber in the OPS architecture was the DB block ping. A DB block ping would occur when an instance participating in an OPS database had a block in its cache required by another participating instance. In OPS, if another instance required the block in the cache of a second instance, the block would have to be written out to disk, the locks transferred, and then the block re-read into the requesting instance.

Oracle 8i OPS implementation brought in many significant changes. The significant new feature was the introduction of cache fusion technology.

Cache fusion, as examined earlier, is a concept where cache, or SGA, from the multiple instances coordinates the buffers and manages the database access.

Oracle 8i (OPS) introduced the initial phase of cache fusion. The data blocks were transferred from the SGA of one instance to the SGA of another instance without the need to write the blocks to disk. This was aimed at reducing the ping overhead of data blocks. However, the partial implementation of cache fusion in Oracle 8i could help only in certain conditions.

RAC Today (10g and 11g)

Oracle 10g RAC

Below is a list of the new features:

- New concept of Service Registration, which aims at helping high availability from the application point of view

- Cluster Ready Service (CRS)

- Oracle Cluster Registry (OCR) for maintaining the configuration information

- Enhancements regarding tools supporting RAC administration – DBCA, SRVCTL, DBUA and Enterprise Manager

- Virtual IP Configuration for a better high availability configuration for the application access

- Limited Rolling upgrade with opatch tool

- Better Workload Management and alignment with Oracle Database Resonance Utility with dynamic provision of the nodes in the cluster

- Web-based Enterprise Manager Database Control with which one can manage a RAC database and Enterprise Manager Grid Control for administering multiple RAC databases

- The Automatic Workload Repository (AWR) to track the performance metrics and provide advice and alerts

Oracle 11g RAC

- Oracle 11g RAC parallel upgrades

- Oracle RAC load balancing advisor

- ADDM for RAC (provides cross-node advisories)

- Interval Partitioning

- ADR (ADRCI) command-line tool (example below)

```
$adrci
adrci> set editor vi
adrci> show alert ( it will open alert in vi editor )
adrci> show alert -tail ( Similar to Unix tail command )
adrci> show alert -tail 200 ( Similar to Unix Command tail -200 )
adrci> show alert -tail -f ( Similar to Unix command tail -f )
```

  - To list all the "ORA-" errors run following command

```
adrci> show alert -P "MESSAGE_TEXT LIKE '%ORA-%'"
```

- Optimized RAC cache fusion protocols

- Oracle 11g RAC Grid provisioning - the Oracle grid control provisioning pack allows one to "blow-out" a RAC node, without the time-consuming install, using a preinstalled "footprint".

- Hot patching

- Quick Fault Resolution

Future of Utility and On-Demand Computing

Utility computing and on-demand computing are here to stay. A May 18, 2008 new datacenter press release from Oracle indicates this.

"Oracle is committed to providing our customers with the highest-level of service, and this new facility in Utah will allow us to support our growing On Demand business, as well as the technology infrastructure to support our research and development and customer service requirements."

Conclusion

The ability of grid computing to perform higher throughput computing, distributing process execution across a parallel infrastructure, brings power—massive computing power—to the people. This chapter gave an introduction to grid computing and its components as well as showing how Oracle is ahead of the game in offering this feature.

References

Source www.ogf.org
http://www.gridtoday.com/grid/432349.html

Cluster and Grid Computing in Japan: Today and in 2010
http://www.gridconsortium.com/grid-consortium-grid-definition.html

http://www.oracle.com/technology/oramag/oracle/05-nov/o65standard.html

http://www.gridwisetech.com/content/view/15/19/lang,en/

http://robertgfreeman.blogspot.com/2007/07/oracle-database-11g-new-feature-to.html

http://viragsharma.blogspot.com/2007/07/how-to-check-alertlog-in-oracle-11g.html

http://www.rittman.net/2006/10/26/oracle-open-world-day-4-11g-performance-scalability-features/

Mark Marshall http://www.linkedin.com/pub/7/3a6/214

RAC Architecture

The Architecture of RAC

In this chapter, the architecture of Oracle 11g RAC is examined in further detail. RAC is a multi-instance single database. The database data files of an Oracle database usually have the .dbf file extension. In RAC, these .dbf data files reside on a shared disk. The shared disk file system must be a cluster aware file system.

One way to better visualize RAC architecture is to redefine what a computer or server is. A typical server has the following components:

- Cabinet /chassis
- Processors/CPUs (Central Processing Units)
- Local hard drives
- Memory/RAM (Random Access Memory)
- System bus

- Public network adapters/Public Ethernet adapters
- Public network link

Additional Server Components for RAC

A server that is part of an Oracle RAC environment has these additional components:

- Shared hard drives
- Cache fusion
- Oracle Clusterware
- Private network adapters / Private Ethernet adapters
- Private network link (InterConnect)

These components will be explained briefly here with cache fusion and clusterware being covered in more detail later in this chapter.

Before shared disks and clustered file systems were a common part of a data center, a computer or server was defined on an individual or discrete basis. Like other clustered systems, Oracle RAC redefines a server. The opposite of individual and discrete is attached, combined, indistinct and joined. The Google search platform is also a clustered system. The hundreds of thousands of computers that make up the Google search platform combine/join together to create one massively powerful server. In the same way, Oracle RAC combines multiple computers to present a single server view to the application and end user.

Cache fusion is a diskless cache coherency mechanism that provides copies of blocks directly from a holding instance's memory cache, or local SGA buffer cache, to a requesting instance's memory cache, or remote SGA buffer cache. A server's local memory communicates with a local CPU via the system or memory bus. In an Oracle RAC environment, the memory bus to CPU communication channel still exists, but the memory communication is extended across the others servers using cache fusion. The memory or cache is fused together across the servers via Gigabit Ethernet, 10 Gigabit Ethernet or the InfiniBand protocol. Gigabit Ethernet's maximum speed is 125 MB/s. 10 Gigabit Ethernet and most InfiniBand implementations are about ten times faster than Gigabit Ethernet.

Oracle Clusterware allows clustering of servers providing the SSI (single system image). Oracle Clusterware is the intelligence in Oracle RAC that ensures the required cooperation between cluster nodes.

A single instance Oracle database can function properly with only one network adapter which is used by the public network. A RAC database with its multiple instances hosted on multiple servers also requires a private network adapter on each server to communicate over the private RAC network. The private RAC network is referred to as the interconnect. This private network link is the communication channel used by cache fusion.

Clusters and Grids Defined

Clusters and grids, which were briefly described in Chapter 1, have a different vision and different objectives. Clusters have static resources for a specific application. Grids, that can consist of multiple clusters and standalone servers, are dynamic resource pools and are shareable among many different applications and users. A grid does not assume that all servers in the grid are running the same set of applications.

RAC Components

At a very high level, RAC architecture consists of these components:

- Physical nodes or hosts
- Physical interconnects and interconnect protocols
- Oracle Clusterware
- Oracle instances and cache fusion

- Shared disk system

- Clustered file system, raw devices, network file system, Automatic Storage Management

- Network services

- Workload Management Services – Virtual IP configuration

A complete Oracle instance consists of disk files, shared memory structures, and background processes. The shared memory area is further subdivided into numerous caches and pools which are used to transfer data, programs, and instructions from processes to and from the disks and users.

Oracle Clusterware

Each of the instances in the cluster configuration communicates with other instances by using the clusterware. Clusterware is the middleware that glues all the clustered instances and projects a single database system image.

Cluster platforms depend on the cluster management program to track the cluster node status. Clusterware allows clustering of servers so that they act as a single system. Clusterware is supported and required on every operating system that is certified for Oracle RAC.

Online Install Guides for Clusterware and RAC

Oracle Clusterware must be installed before installing the Oracle database software. Below are the URLs of two excellent click–by-click Oracle 11g RAC install guides. Thanks to Jeff Hunter and Tim Hall for all their hard work to provide these excellent resources. Jeff's guide prints out to be over 130 pages!

Jeff Hunter's install guide:
http://www.idevelopment.info/data/Oracle/DBA_tips/Oracle11gRAC /CLUSTER_10.shtml

Tim Hall's install guide:
http://www.oracle-base.com/articles/11g/OracleDB11gR1RACInstallationOnLinuxUsingNFS.php

Oracle Clusterware was released with Oracle 10g and was known as CRS. The product was renamed to Oracle Clusterware in version Oracle 10g R2. Proving that the rename of CRS to Clusterware was more marketing than anything, the reference to the Clusterware home directory still uses the name CRS_HOME.

Oracle Clusterware Explained

From Oracle:

> "In the event of a system failure, clustering ensures high availability to users. A redundant hardware component, such as additional nodes, interconnects, and disks, allow the cluster to provide high availability. Such redundant hardware architectures avoid single points-of-failure and provide exceptional fault resilience.

In Real Application Cluster environments, Oracle Clusterware monitors and manages Real Application Cluster (RAC) databases. When a node in a cluster is started, all instances, services and listeners are started automatically. If an instance fails, the clusterware will restart the instance so the service is often restored before the administrator notices it was down.

"In this sense, Oracle Clusterware is the basis for Oracle Real Application Clusters. Therefore, there needs to be one incarnation of the Oracle Clusterware on every node of the cluster that an Oracle RAC Database Instance is supposed to run on." (Quoted from Oracle)

Additionally, Clusterware provides node monitoring for the other nodes in the system via a heartbeat signal sent over the cluster interconnect. All nodes in a RAC cluster keep track of which nodes are available.

The shared storage provides concurrent access by all the cluster nodes to the storage array. The storage array is presented in the form of logical units (LUNS) to the cluster host or node and the file system is mounted on all nodes. Thus, when the same file system is mounted and used on all nodes in the cluster, it is called a cluster file system.

Oracle 10g and 11g provides a flexible and high performing shared storage methodology that is known as Automatic Storage Management (ASM). ASM may be used in lieu of the cluster file system.

Oracle Clusterware is required

As stated by Oracle's documentation, "Oracle Clusterware is a requirement for using Oracle 11g RAC, and it is the only clusterware that you need for most platforms. Although Oracle 11g RAC continues to support select third-party clusterware products on specific platforms, you MUST also install and use Oracle Clusterware."

The Oracle Universal Installer (OUI) installs clusterware on each node. The clusterware home is called CRS home. The CRS home is distinct from the RAC-enabled Oracle home. The CRS home can be shared by one or more nodes, or be private to each node. Vendor clusterware may be installed with Oracle Clusterware for all UNIX-based operating systems except Linux.

The Oracle Cluster Registry (OCR) contains cluster and database configuration information for RAC Cluster Ready Services (CRS), including the list of nodes in the cluster database, the CRS application, resource profiles, and the authorizations for the Event Manager (EVM). The OCR can reside in a file on a cluster file system or on a shared raw device. Raw devices will not be supported in future versions of Oracle (Metalink 578455.1).

Clusterware Features

The clusterware software is installed in the cluster with its own set of binaries. The CRS Home and Oracle Home are in different locations.

The clusterware software installs both the Voting Disk file and the OCR file. Installation of clusterware configures the Virtual IP interface. CRS resources can also be managed by the srvctl utility.

Clusterware has many daemon processes. They are as follows:

- **CRDS** – The CRS Daemon is the main background process for managing the HA operation of the service. It manages the application resources defined within the cluster. It also maintains the configuration profiles stored in the Oracle Configuration Repository. Process will restart upon failure.

- **OCSSD** – Process that manages the Cluster Synchronization Services (CSS) daemon. Manages cluster node membership and runs as oracle user. Failure of this process results in cluster restart. Failure of OCSSD causes a node restart.

- **EVMD** – This is event management logger. It monitors the message flow between the nodes and logs the relevant event information to the log files.

- **OPROCD** – Cluster process monitor. This process only runs on platforms that do not use added third-party vendor clusterware.

Cluster Private Interconnect

The cluster private interconnect is a high bandwidth, low latency communication facility that connects each node to other nodes in the cluster and routes messages among the nodes. It is a key component in building the RAC system.

The Oracle RAC cluster interconnect is used for the following high-level functions:

- Monitoring Health, Status, and Synchronize messages

- Transporting lock management or resource coordination messages

- Moving the cache buffers (data blocks) from node to node

High performance database computing involves distributing the processing across an array of cluster nodes. It requires that the cluster interconnect provide high-data rates and low-latency communication between node processes.

The interconnect technology that is employed while connecting RAC Nodes should be scalable to handle the amount of traffic generated by the cache synchronization mechanism. This is directly related to the amount of contention created by the application. The more inter-instance updates and inter-instance transfers there are, the more message traffic generated. It is advisable to implement the highest bandwidth/lowest latency interconnect that is available for a given platform. If the server vendor and budget supports it, consider InfiniBand or 10 Gigabit Ethernet.

The volume of synchronization traffic directly impacts the bandwidth requirement. The interconnect is not something that should be under configured.

The next section will help define the difference between a database and database instance. Understanding the difference is important in order to appreciate Oracle RAC.

Database and Database Instance

Oracle Database Server represents a collection of physical files, logical database objects such as tables and indexes, and the host level memory structures and processes. The physical host level files reside on storage arrays, directly attached, network attached, or on a storage area network (SAN). The combination of background processes and memory buffers is called the database instance. An Oracle database instance, which resides on a host, is the actual database processing area that allows access to the physical and logical structures.

A RAC database consists of multiple database instances. Access to the database (dbf files) is shared by the multiple instances. In other words, the database consists of a single set of physical data files that can be accessed by multiple database instances.

As shown in Figure 2.1, each of the instances resides on a separate host and forms its own set of background processes and memory buffers. Thus, RAC enables access to a single database via multiple database instances.

instance_name vs. db_name

When the database is not a RAC system, it has one instance and one database. Sometimes, the instance and database are construed to be the same. In that case, it is called a standalone database system.

As an example,

```
Database Name       : NYDB50

Instance-1 Name     : NYDB51
Instance-2 Name     : NYDB52
Instance-3 Name     : NYDB53
```

The parameter *db_name* will have the value of NYDB50; this represents the name of the database. The parameter *instance_name* will be one of the names listed above. All of these instances provide access to the same database named NYDB50.

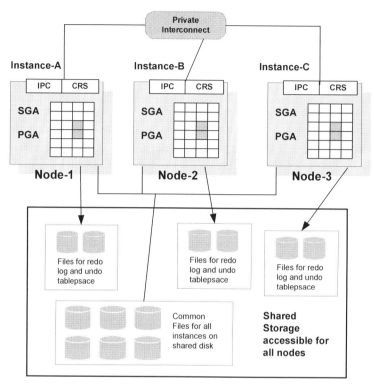

Figure 2.1: *Multi-Instance RAC Database System – At a Glance*

Database Instance

A typical RAC instance is similar to a stand-alone instance. A RAC instance has extra processes, memory structures, and logical structures. Since RAC must maintain concurrency of data across multiple instances, it creates additional structures to manage and coordinate the resources.

System Global Area (SGA)

The SGA components include the database buffer cache, large pool, java pool, streams pool, redo log buffer and the shared pool. The main memory structures of the shared pool are the dictionary cache, library cache and the result cache. Unlike the PGA, the SGA memory structures are shared.

The SGA and PGA memory structures are shown in the Figure 2.2. The SGA resources are formed at the time of database instance launch based on the instance initialization parameters. However, many of the parameters can dynamically be altered to suit the database processing needs.

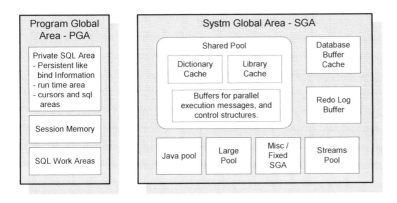

Figure 2.2: *SGA and PGA Components of a Typical Instance*

Database Buffer Cache

The database buffer cache holds copies of the data blocks read from the data files. Access to the database buffer cache is shared.

From Oracle version 8 onwards, the buffer cache contains three buffer pools for different types of data usage. They are DEFAULT, KEEP, and RECYCLE. These three buffer pools have separate allocations of buffers and LRU lists that manage buffers.

- The RECYCLE buffer pool is used to store blocks that are virtually never used after the initial read

- The KEEP pool is for blocks that are referenced frequently

- The DEFAULT buffer pool contains objects that are not assigned to any buffer pool and objects that are explicitly assigned to the DEFAULT pool. Direct insert and direct read operations used for data loading, sorting, or hashing operations bypass buffer pools.

In Oracle 11g RAC, the database block buffers from each instance, through cache fusion, are merged to form a massive logical database buffer cache.

Large Pool

The large pool is an optional memory area in the SGA. This separate memory area is beneficial for memory intensive tasks such as backup and restore operations.

JAVA Pool

The JAVA Pool holds the JAVA execution code in a similar manner to the PL/SQL cache in the shared pool. The JAVA pool is used by many internal routines.

Streams Pool

The streams pool is used exclusively by Oracle Streams. To configure the streams pool explicitly, specify the size of the pool in bytes using the *streams_pool_size* initialization parameter. If the size of the streams pool is zero or not specified, then the memory used by streams is allocated from the shared pool.

Redo Log Buffers

Redo log buffers are used to hold the redo records generated by each data changing transaction. The redo log buffer is a circular buffer. Redo entries contain the steps needed to reconstruct changes made to the database by UPDATE, INSERT, CREATE, DELETE, ALTER, and DROP operations. A redo log buffer is written out to the online redo log by the log writer process when:

- The buffer becomes one third full
- Three seconds have elapsed
- When a DBWn process writes modified buffers to disk
- On commit record - when a user process commits a transaction

While it is possible to have different sized redo log buffers and redo logs on each instance in a RAC database, this is not a suggested configuration. It can lead to confusion and misunderstanding during recovery operations. Each instance in a RAC database must have its own thread of redo logs.

Shared Pool

The shared pool holds the dictionary cache, library cache, result cache, message queues, latch and lock areas, buffers for parallel execution messages, and control structures.

The data dictionary is a collection of internal tables and views of reference information about the database, the structure and users.
The dictionary cache is the memory area designated to hold dictionary data. It is also known as the row cache because it holds data as rows instead of buffers that hold entire blocks of data.

The library cache includes the shared SQL areas, PL/SQL procedures and packages, and control structures such as locks and library cache handles.

Fixed SGA

A portion of the SGA contains general information about the state of the database and the instance, which the background processes need to access. This is called the fixed SGA. No user data is stored here. The SGA also includes information communicated between processes, such as locking information.

Automatic Shared Memory Management

Automatic Shared Memory Management (ASMM) adjusts the sizes of the SGA components on the fly as the workload changes. Automatic Shared Memory Management (ASMM), a 10g and 11g feature, is meant to simplify SGA management. Do not confuse ASMM with AMM

(Automatic Memory Management). ASMM was introduced in Oracle 10g. AMM is new in 11g and will be addressed in this chapter.

The DBA specifies the amount of memory available to an instance via the *sga_target* parameter. The Oracle database periodically redistributes memory between the components according to workload requirements. This solves the allocation issues that are normally faced when using the manual method. Under-sizing memory settings can lead to poor performance and out-of memory errors (ORA-4031).

If a non-zero value is specified for *sga_target*, the following six memory pools are automatically sized by Oracle:

- Database buffer cache (Only the default pool)

- Shared pool

- Large pool

- Java pool

- Streams pool

- Fixed SGA and other internal allocations

Figure 2.3 shows an example of auto-tuned SGA components.

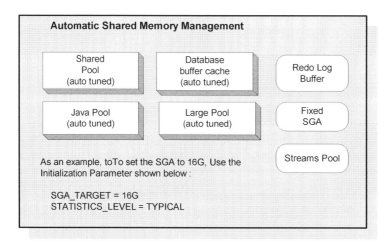

Figure 2.3: *SGA Memory Buffers Managed Dynamically Using ASMM*

When using ASMM, configuration of the following buffers remains manual:

- Log buffer
- KEEP/RECYCLE buffer caches
- Nonstandard block size buffer caches

When *sga_target* is set, the total size of manual SGA parameters are subtracted from the *sga_target* value and the balance is given to the auto-tuned SGA components.

Sga_target is also a dynamic parameter and can be changed through Enterprise Manager or with the ALTER SYSTEM command. However, the *sga_target* can be increased only up to the value of *sga_max_size*.

Important: *statistics_level* must be set to TYPICAL (default) or ALL to use Automatic Shared Memory Management.

Program Global Area (PGA)

A Program Global Area (PGA) is a memory region that stores the data and control information for the server processes. Each server process has a non-shared memory region created by Oracle when a server process is started. Access to the PGA is exclusive to that server process, and it is read and written only by Oracle code. Broadly speaking, PGA contains a private SQL area and a session memory area.

A private SQL area contains data such as bind information and runtime memory structures. Each session that issues a SQL statement has a private SQL area. Session memory is the memory allocated to hold a session's variables, logon information, and other information related to the session.

With the initialization parameter *pga_aggregate_target*, sizing of work areas for all dedicated sessions is made automatic, and all *_area_size* parameters are ignored for these sessions.

Automatic Memory Management

Oracle Database 11g can routinely manage both the SGA and PGA. Using this method, the database automatically tunes the sizes of the individual SGA components and the sizes of the individual PGAs.

New in 11g, Automatic Memory Management (AMM) enables the Oracle Database to automatically manage the instance memory. Sophisticated algorithms are used to adjust SGA and PGA memory settings as needs change. Oracle strongly recommends using AMM. Once the *memory_target* parameter has been set, then, in theory, one can forget about it. AMM is the simplest way to manage memory. AMM is available for Linux, Solaris, Windows, HP-UX, and AIX.

The main difference between ASMM and AMM is that AMM can manage SGA and PGA settings. ASMM can only manage the SGA. During installation, AMM is enabled if the basic install options are used.

The additional RAC SGA areas are the Global Cache Service (GCS) and Global Enqueue Service (GES) and are collections of background processes. Both of these processes cover and manage the total cache fusion process, resource transfers, and resource escalations among the instances.

GES and GCS together maintain a Global Resource Directory (GRD) to record the status of each cached block. GRD remains in memory and is stored on all the instances. Each instance manages a portion of the directory. This distributed nature is a key point for fault tolerance of the RAC.

Global Resource Directory (GRD) is the internal database that records and stores the status of the data blocks. Whenever a block is transferred out of a local cache to another instance's cache, the GRD is updated. The following resource information is available in the GRD:

- Data Block Identifiers (DBA)

- Location of most current version
- Modes of the data blocks: (N) Null, (S) Shared, (X) Exclusive
- The roles of the data blocks (local or global) held by each instance
- Buffer caches on multiple nodes in the cluster

The GRD keeps track of the inventory of resources and their status and location.

The Background Processes

This next section covers the processes. Background processes are spawned to execute the database processing. The following is a description of each of the background processes:

- **SMON** - System Monitor process performs recovery after instance failure and monitors temporary segments and extents. SMON can also perform instance recovery for other failed RAC instances.

- **PMON** - Process Monitor recovers failed user process resources. PMON performs cleanup of user process resources such as releasing locks.

- **DBWR** - Database Writer or Dirty Buffer Writer are responsible for writing dirty buffers from the database block cache to the database data files. Generally, DBWR only writes blocks back to the data files on commit, or when the cache is full and space has to be made for more blocks. The DBWR processes in RAC must be coordinated through the locking and global cache processes to ensure efficient processing is accomplished. Oracle 11g allows for a maximum of 20 DBWR processes.

- **LGWR** - Log Writer process is responsible for writing the log buffers out to the redo logs. In RAC, each RAC instance has its own LGWR process that maintains that instance's thread of redo logs. Redo log entries are written sequentially.

- **ARCH** - (Optional). When running in ARCHIVELOG mode, the archive process writes filled redo logs to the archive log location(s).

The archive log files are critical for RAC and non-RAC database recovery.

- **CKPT** - A database checkpoint is a method where the state of a database is saved. The checkpoint process writes checkpoint information to control files and data file headers. Remember that the checkpoint process is the manager of the database checkpoint; the actual writing of blocks to disk is done by DBWR.

- **CJQ0** - Job queue controller process wakes up periodically and checks the JOB$ table. If a job is due, it spawns Jnnn processes to handle jobs. A failure of this process does not cause an instance failure.

- **Jnnn** - Job processes used by the job queues to process jobs. The CJQ0 process controls it automatically.

- **QMN** - (Optional). Advanced Queuing process for Oracle Streams. A failure of this process does not cause an instance failure.

- **ASMB** - ASM bridge process. Process used for RDBMS instance to ASM instance communication such as data file adding or removing.

- **DBRM** - Database resource manager process. Handles resource manager related tasks.

- **DIA0** - Diagnosability process responsible for hang detection and deadlock resolution.

- **DIAG** - Diagnosability process that performs diagnostic dumps and executes global oradebug commands.

- **EMNC** - Event monitor coordinator. A process used for database event management and notifications.

- **FBDA** - Flashback data archiver process. Archives rows of tracked tables to flashback data archive. Inserts are not archived.

- **FMON** – The database communicates with the mapping libraries provided by storage vendors through an external non-Oracle database process that is spawned by a background process called FMON. FMON is responsible for managing the mapping information. When the *file_mapping* initialization parameter is specified for mapping data files to physical devices on a storage subsystem, the FMON process is spawned.

- **GMON** - Maintains disk membership in ASM disk groups

- **KATE** - Konductor of ASM temporary errands. Complete proxy I/O to ASM metafile when disk goes offline.

- **MARK** - "Marks" ASM allocation units stale during a failed write to disk that is offline. An allocation unit is the smallest contiguous disk space in ASM.

- **MMAN** - Used for internal database tasks

- **MMNL** – This process performs frequent and lightweight manageability related tasks such as session history capture and metrics computation.

- **MMON** – This process performs various manageability-related background tasks, for example:

  - Issuing alerts whenever a given metric violates its threshold value

  - Taking snapshots

  - Capturing statistics values for SQL objects which have been recently modified

- **PSP0** - Spawns Oracle processes

- **RBAL** - Manages rebalance activity for ASM disk groups

- **ARBn** - ASM Rebalance process. Completes the actual rebalance work.

- **SMCO** - Space management coordinator. Involves proactive space allocation and reclaiming. Spawns Wnnn processes to do its work.

- **VKTM** - Virtual keeper of time

The RAC database has the same processes as that of a single-instance Oracle database. However, there are additional RAC specific processes. Those processes will be examined in the next section.

RAC Specific Background Processes

The following are the additional processes spawned for supporting the multi-instance coordination:

- **LMON** - The Global Enqueue Service Monitor (LMON) monitors the entire cluster to manage the global Enqueues and the resources. LMON manages instance and process failures and the associated recovery for the Global Cache Service (GCS) and Global Enqueue Service (GES). In particular, LMON handles the part of recovery associated with global resources. LMON-provided services are also known as cluster group services.

- **LMD** - Global Enqueue Service Daemon. The LMD process manages incoming remote resource requests on each instance.

- **LMS** - The LMSn processes handle the blocking interrupts from the remote instance for the Global Cache Service resources by:

    - managing the resource requests and cross-instance call operations for the shared resources

    - building a list of invalid lock elements and validating the lock elements during recovery

    - handling the global lock deadlock detection and monitoring for the lock conversion timeouts

- **LCK0** - Instance Enqueue Process

- **RMSn** – Oracle RAC Management Processes. Manage tasks for RAC such as creation of resources when new RAC instances are added.

- **RSMS** – Remote Slave Monitor manages background slave process creation and communication on remote instances

- **ACMS** - Atomic Controlfile to Memory Service process that helps to ensure data integrity. Ensures a SGA update is globally committed or globally aborted in an Oracle RAC system.

- **GTX0-J** - Global transaction processes that provide support for XA global transactions in Oracle RAC. XA is an industry standard specification for distributed transaction processing.

Cache Fusion Background Processes

Global Cache Service

The Global Cache Service (GCS) is the main controlling process that implements cache fusion. GCS keeps track of the block mode for blocks in the global role. GCS controls block transfers between instances, ensuring complete data integrity. As requests are made from a remote instance, GCS organizes the block shipping and appropriate lock mode conversions. The Global Cache Service is implemented by various background processes such as the Global Cache Service Processes (LMSn) and Global Enqueue Service Daemon (LMD).

Global Enqueue Service

The Global Enqueue Service (GES) manages or tracks the status of all the enqueues that are shared globally.

All the memory structures and background processes have now been surveyed. The physical database structures of the database include the data files, redo log files and control files among other type of files.

Database Related Files

Oracle database is a collection of physical files. These are the operating system files used by the database and database instance. Oracle RAC needs shared storage to store the files. RAC follows the shared disk model where all the cluster nodes share the same disk or storage volumes. This is called a "shared-everything" cluster.

The files included in the RAC architecture are shown in Figure 2.4. Most of them must be available simultaneously and be updateable by all the nodes/instances in the cluster. Some files can remain on the local file system.

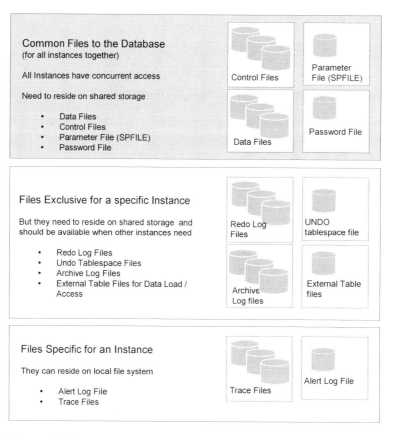

Figure 2.4: *Database Related Files*

Data Files

These .dbf files are the main files of the database. The data files contain the actual data. The logical database structures like tables and indexes are physically stored in the data files. In RAC, these files are located on shared storage and are accessible by all the nodes in the cluster. One or more data files form a logical unit of database storage called the tablespace.

Data files can be associated with multiple instances but only one database. By locating the data files either on a clustered file system, a network file system, or a raw partition, they are made accessible by all the nodes.

Control Files

The control files contain entries that specify the physical structure of the database. This small binary file is continuously updated when a database instance is online. The control files contain the key information such as the database name, name and location of the data files, and redo log files for the database.

When an instance is launched, the control files identify the data and redo log files. Control files should be multiplexed and located on the shared storage.

Redo Log Files

Oracle defines the redo log as the most crucial structure for recovery operations. A redo log is made up of redo entries that are also called redo records. The primary function of the redo log is to record all changes made to data. In a high update database, moving the redo logs to separate disks is advised. Every database has a set of redo log files. The information in the redo log files is used to recover the database from a system or media failure. There are generally two or more redo log files. They are used by the database in a circular fashion. Once a redo log file is filled up, then the next redo log file is picked up for writing. Meanwhile, the filled redo log file is saved as an archived log file.

Redo log files are stored as a group called Redo Log File groups. Each group can have one or more redo log files. Multiplexing the redo files within a group provides a higher level of resiliency and job security.

Redo log files are instance specific. In the RAC database architecture, each instance has its own set of redo log file groups. Even though they are specific to an individual instance, the redo log files need to be located on shared storage for recovery purposes. Another important use of redo logs is hot mining of redo log files by Oracle streams where redo log files are scanned in order to propagate the changes to other Oracle database systems.

Archive Log Files

Archive log files are actually the saved redo log files. When a redo log file is filled up and the next redo log file is put to use, the filled redo log file is saved or archived. The saved files are known as archive log files.

Automatic archiving can be enabled on the redo log. Oracle automatically archives redo log files when the database in is in ARCHIVELOG mode. The archive logs are written to the destination specified by the *log_archive_dest* parameter and the optional *log_archive_duplex_dest* parameter. If sending the archived log files to a remote destination is required, then the *log_archive_dest_n* parameter would be used where n is an integer from 1 to 10. The *log_archive_dest_n* parameter supports both local and remote destinations. The *log_archive_dest* and *log_archive_duplex_dest* only support local destinations.

In RAC, a separate set of archive log files is created by each instance. Since each RAC instance has its own redo log files, the corresponding archive log files are produced when the log switch takes place. The archive log files may be written to a local file system or to a cluster file system. Oracle does not insist upon a particular type of file system. Writing to a clustered file system has the added advantage of being available to archive all the nodes in the cluster, which becomes important in case of media recovery.

Parameter File (SPFILE)

The attributes of an instance depend on the initialization parameters used for starting up the instance. Initialization parameters control the configuration of the database system. They are the key directives to start and manage any instance. While launching the database instance, parameters are specified, and they remain until the instance is shutdown.

Optionally, certain parameters may be modified during the instance run time by the ALTER SYSTEM SET method, provided the instance has been started with the SPFILE method.

The SPFILE feature allows the changing of parameter values dynamically. It also allows them to be set either permanently or in memory only. For Oracle Real Application Clusters (RAC), one server parameter file can be used and shared among instances. The usage of a single copy of the SPFILE for the entire database provides administrative convenience and simplification. The SPFILE must be located on a clustered file system.

Password File

The password file is another important file that is shared by all the instances of Oracle 11g RAC. This file, which is stored in binary format, records all of the authentication privileges granted to the users. Privileges such as SYSDBA or SYSOPER are recorded in this file. The password file is required for remote authentication for the users with SYSDBA or SYSOPER privileges. This file is located on the shared file system.

Alert Log File and Trace Files

In Oracle 11g, alert and trace files are stored in the Automatic Diagnostic Repository (ADR). ADR is a fault diagnosability infrastructure for preventing, detecting, diagnosing, and resolving problems. The problem categories are database code bugs, metadata corruption, and user data corruption. Oracle 11g maintains two alert log files: a text formatted and XML formatted file. The alert log file, background trace files, and server process trace files are created in the ADR. The new 11g *diagnostic_dest* parameter determines the ADR location.

Each instance in the RAC database writes to the alert log file and produces trace files periodically. The alert log file contains all of the messages generated by the Oracle database kernel. Trace files contain detailed information about a specific event or issue. These log and trace files help the administrators keep track of the database activity and assist in troubleshooting. Upon instance startup, the database writes all non-default parameter settings to the alert log file.

The alter log file and trace files may be written either to a directory within a local file system or within the cluster file system.

Files for Loading into External Tables

External tables allow direct access of data located in the operating system level files by using the SQL interface within the database. It is a way of reading and writing files into and out of the database. Note that one cannot write to an existing external table. Data stored in operating system level files (ASCII filer) can be accessed as if they are a table with rows and columns. Joins and views can be constructed with data in the O/S file and logical database tables.

For all practical purposes, external tables act the same as the usual tables; however, the data is not stored with the Oracle data files. External tables are a great way to load the data into a database and do data processing. Inserts, updates, and index creation are not allowed on an external table. A DROP TABLE statement issued against an external table removes the table metadata only; the operating system file is not removed.

There is no restriction as to where the external table data file has to be located. In a RAC database system, it can be located on the local file system or on shared disk. For the sake of concurrent access, it becomes more meaningful to keep the external table file on a shared storage. This allows for transparent access to the external table so that any instance in the RAC database should be able to read it at the operating system level (ASCII). This is possible only if the external table file is located on a shared disk.

Oracle Cluster Registry (OCR)

The OCR contains cluster and database configuration information for RAC and Cluster Ready Services (CRS) such as the cluster node list, instance to node mapping, and CRS application resource profiles.

The OCR is a shared file located in a cluster file system. When not using a cluster file system, the OCR file can be located on a shared raw device in UNIX-based systems or a shared logical partition in Windows environments. If more than one database is created on the cluster, they all share the same Oracle cluster registry.

Voting Disk

The voting disk file must reside on shared storage. The voting disk file manages information for node membership. Oracle recommends using multiple voting disk files.

ORACLE_HOME Files (Oracle Binaries)

Typically, every instance in Oracle 11g RAC will have its own ORACLE_HOME and a set of exclusive binaries. However, the Oracle binaries are located either on a local file system or on a clustered file system. Locating the Oracle home (binaries) on a clustered file system provides easier management by keeping a single copy of Oracle home supporting all the instances.

A common Oracle home for multiple instances has some advantages because it helps to easily expand the nodes and shrink the nodes as needed. It helps the dynamic addition and expansion of nodes without bothering with a fresh install of the Oracle binaries for the new instance. This feature is useful for large clusters, and it fits into the grid strategy of easier addition and reduction of computing resources.

UNDO Tablespace Files

UNDO tablespaces are special tablespaces that have system undo segments. They contain before images of blocks involved in uncommitted transactions. As such, they are the primary support structure allowing a transaction to rollback if the decision is made to not commit the transaction. Tables and indexes cannot be created in the undo tablespace. A database can have more than one undo tablespace, but only one can be used at one time. Automatic undo management is the default mode for an 11g database. DBCA will automatically create an undo tablespace named UNDOTBS1.

RAW Partitions, Cluster File System and Automatic Storage Management (ASM)

Oracle RAC database files are located on shared storage units. Shared storage disks are physically connected to all of the nodes. All of the nodes need to have read and write access concurrently to the data devices. The presentation of the data devices to the operating systems can be achieved either by raw partitions or through the cluster file system. A raw partition is a disk drive device that does not have a file system set up. The raw partition is a portion of the physical disk that is accessed at the lowest possible level. The actual application that uses a raw device is responsible for managing its own I/O to the raw device with no operating system buffering.

Oracle 10g and 11g RAC support shares storage resources located in the ASM instance. The ASM resources are sharable and accessed by all the nodes in the RAC system.

Storage occupies an important place in the overall architecture of the RAC system. It is crucial to plan and design carefully to get the right storage array in a compatible environment.

Concept of Redo Thread

In the RAC system, each instance must have its own redo log groups. The redo log file groups of an instance are collectively called a thread. Each instance has its own redo log thread. The redo log groups function in a true circular fashion; as one fills up, another redo log records the redo entries. In a stand-alone instance, there is only one thread. In a RAC system, typically there are as many threads as instances. The thread number identifies each thread. The threads may have different numbers of redo groups, but each group must have at least two members, as shown in Figure 2.5.

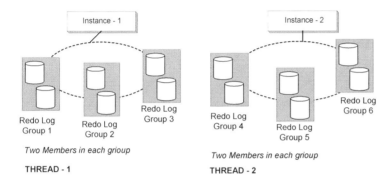

Figure 2.5: *Redo Threads in a 2-Node RAC Database*

Online redo logs record the redo entries as transactions commit and rollback. Redo groups may optionally have additional members to provide mirroring of the redo groups.

Thread Features

Each instance must have a minimum of two redo groups with each group having at least one member in the group. Every redo group has a group number, which is a unique number in the database. All of the redo log files supporting the redo groups reside on shared storage so that every instance in the cluster can access all of the redo groups during the recovery process. As shown in Figure 2.6, all of the redo groups are located on a shared storage unit.

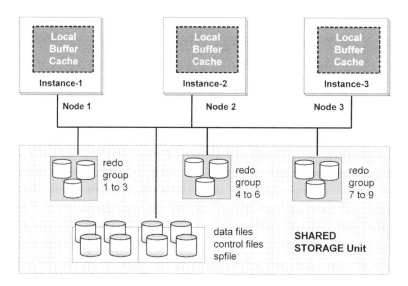

Figure 2.6: *Redo Groups on a Shared Storage*

Use a minimum of three redo groups in a thread. Keep at least two redo members for each redo group for multiplexing and protection. Multiplexing the redo members is optional but is highly recommended. Different degrees of mirroring are permitted in different threads.

Database Logical Objects

The logical storage structures include, at the lowest level, the data blocks, and at the next level, the extents. A group of extents set aside for a specific object is grouped into a segment. At the highest level is the tablespace.

The Oracle data rows are stored in data blocks. A data block is the smallest or most granular basic logical structure that is brought into the buffer cache from disk storage in order to do SQL processing. The standard size of the data block is specified by the *db_block_size* initialization parameter. Up to five other block sizes can be specified. The data block size for performance reasons must be a multiple of the operating system block size to avoid unnecessary I/O.

The next level of logical database structure is an extent. An extent is a specific number of contiguous data blocks, which are obtained in a single allocation unit.

A segment is a set of extents allocated for a certain logical structure. There are many types of segments, namely: data segments, index segments, temporary segments, and undo segments.

Tablespaces

At the highest level of the logical structure chain is the tablespace. It is a logical administrative unit and is composed of many Oracle data files. Within the tablespace area, the extents are created which are assigned to the segments. Structures like tables and indexes are created out of the tablespace.

The traditional tablespace is referred to as a smallfile tablespace (SFT). A smallfile tablespace contains multiple, relatively small files. However, with the 10g release, a new concept of bigfile tablespace (BFT) was introduced. A BFT tablespace contains a single file that can have a very large size. The bigfile tablespace has the following characteristics:

- An Oracle database can contain both bigfile and smallfile tablespaces
- System default is to create the traditional smallfile tablespace
- The SYSTEM and SYSAUX tablespaces are always created using the system default type
- Bigfile tablespaces are supported only for locally managed tablespaces with automatic segment-space management

There are two exceptions when bigfile tablespace segments are managed manually:

- locally managed undo tablespace
- temporary tablespace

Bigfile tablespaces are intended to be used with Automated Storage Management (ASM) or other logical volume managers that support

RAID. However, they can also be used without ASM. Bigfile tablespace benefits are as follows:

- It simplifies large database tablespace management by reducing the number of data files needed

- It simplifies data file management with Oracle-managed files and Automated Storage Management (ASM) by eliminating the need for adding new data files and dealing with multiple files

- It allows the creation of a bigfile tablespace of up to eight exabytes (eight million terabytes) in size and significantly increases the storage capacity of an Oracle database

- It follows the concept that a tablespace and a data file are logically equivalent

- It provides the maximum database size

Cache Fusion

The topics that will be covered in this section include the nature, internals, and working mechanism of cache fusion technology along with the following subjects:

- Virtualization of multiple caches into a single cache

- How the data blocks are moved across among multiple SGAs in a multi-node environment

- Synchronization of resource access

- Resource coordination methodology

- Re-mastering of resources in the event of unforeseen failure of any instance

Cache fusion is a diskless cache coherency mechanism that provides copies of blocks directly from a holding instance's memory cache (local SGA buffer cache) to a requesting instance's memory cache (remote SGA buffer cache).

A RAC system equipped with low-latency and high speed interconnect technology enables the buffer cache of each node in the cluster to fuse and form into a single virtual global cache, hence the term cache fusion. The cache fusion architecture creates a shared-cache and provides a single cache image or view to the applications. Internals are transparent to the applications.

From a functional viewpoint, an instance in a RAC system is equivalent to a single instance of Oracle. The extension of multiple cache buffers into a single fused global cache improves scalability, reliability, and availability.

While cache fusion provides Oracle users with an expanded database cache for queries and updates of I/O operations, the improved performance depends greatly on the efficiency of the inter-node message passing mechanism that handles the data block transfers.

Evolution of Cache Fusion

Before looking deeper into the implementation of cache fusion in Oracle 11g RAC, some time needs to be taken to look at the implementation in the 8i release. Oracle Release 8i (Oracle Parallel Server) introduced the initial phase of cache fusion. The data blocks were transferred from the SGA of one instance to the SGA of another instance without the need to write the blocks to disk. This was aimed at reducing the ping overhead of data blocks. However, the partial implementation of cache fusion in 8i could help only in certain conditions, as indicated in Table 2.1.

REQUESTING INSTANCE	HOLDING INSTANCE	DIRTY BLOCK EXISTS IN HOLDING INSTANCE	CACHE COHERENCY METHOD
For Read	Read	Yes	Cache Fusion
For Read	Write	No	Soft Ping (read from disk)

For Read	Write	Yes	Cache Fusion
For Write	Write	Does Not matter	Ping (force disk write)

Table 2.1: *The Methods of Maintaining Cache Coherency*

Oracle 8i (Oracle Parallel Server) had a background process called the Block Server Process (BSP), which facilitated cache fusion. BSP was responsible for transferring the required blocks directly from the owning instance to the buffer cache of the requested instance.

For read/write operations, if the block was already written to disk by the holding instance, the requested block was read from the disk. It involved a soft ping or an I/O-less ping. If the block was available on the holding instance buffer, the BSP process prepared a consistent read (CR) image of the data block. It was then sent to the requesting instance.

A write/write operation invariably involved the ping of the data block. When the ping occurred, the holding instance wrote to disk and downgraded the lock mode. Then, the requesting instance acquired the necessary lock mode and read from the disk. This frequent pinging hurt the performance of the OPS database. With the full implementation of cache fusion in release 9i, 10g, and 11g, all these ping, soft ping, and false ping issues have been solved. Cache fusion now fully resolves write/write conflicts using the new architecture of resource coordination and global cache service.

Nature of Cache Fusion

Multi-node Oracle RAC systems are comprised of multiple instances with each instance residing on an individual node or server. Each Oracle instance in the cluster has a dedicated set of memory structures including background processes and system global areas (SGA) that exist irrespective of another node's instance. Thus, each node's instance has its local buffer cache. When applications or users connect and process their SQL operations, they connect to one of the nodes. When the user processes fetch and access data blocks, the scope of such activity is confined to the SGA of the connected instance.

As the database is mounted with multiple instances, data blocks may exist on any of the instances or any instance may fetch the data blocks as needed by the user processes. In other words, when a user process is looking for a set of data blocks to satisfy the SQL operation requirement, the same set of blocks or some of the blocks may already be available in another node's instance. This highlights an important fact of a RAC system. As opposed to a single stand-alone Oracle instance, there are multiple server locations in a RAC system where data blocks reside. Thus, there are several cache buffers dealing with the same physical database objects.

This is where the method of cache fusion plays a key role. For all practical purposes, multiple buffer caches join and act as if they were a single entity. As shown in Figure 2.7, cache buffers from three nodes are fused together to form a single entity and share data blocks. Maintaining consistency among the cached versions of data blocks in multiple instances is called cache coherency. Cache fusion treats multiple buffer caches as one global cache, solving data consistency issues internally, without any impact on the application code or design.

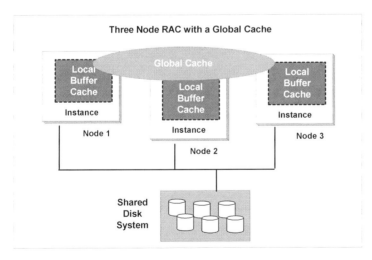

Figure 2.7: *Global Cache – Cache Fusion in a Three-Node Cluster*

Benefits of Cache Fusion

Oracle RAC, with its multiple instances, is able to provide more resources through multiple system global areas (SGA). Cache fusion technology makes it easier to process a very high number of concurrent users and SQL operations without compromising data consistency. It adheres to Oracle's multi-version consistency model and ensures data integrity and data consistency across the instances.

Cache fusion creates an environment where users are able to utilize any instance in the cluster without giving undue preference for a particular instance. There is no need for the extra effort of partitioning data access across nodes, as required in earlier versions of parallel servers. Load balancing is more effective in such an environment.

As a result, very high scalability of database performance can be achieved simply by adding nodes to the cluster. RAC also enables better database capacity planning and conserves capital investment by consolidating many databases on a single large database, thus reducing administrative overhead.

A scalable application on a single-node Oracle server will be just as flexible on a multi-node RAC, even in different workload situations. However, scalability performance may be better with a workload of minimal cross-instance block transfers (OLTP operations) compared to a workload of large cross-instance block transfers. Where there is a large cross-instance transfer of resources, there is a certain overhead due to lock conversions and block transfers from one cache to another.

The advantage of improved load balancing can be used to leverage application performance. User connections can randomly access any instance in the cluster. Contention for server resources, such as the CPU and memory, is reduced.

Concurrency and Consistency

Database systems provide data concurrency by enabling multiple users to access the same data without compromising data consistency. Data consistency means that each user sees a consistent view of the data, including the visible changes made by the users' own transactions, as well as the transactions of other users. Oracle automatically supplies a query with read-consistent data so that all data that the query sees comes from a single point in time (statement-level read consistency).

Optionally, Oracle can provide read consistency to all queries in a transaction (transaction-level read consistency). Oracle maintains undo records to manage such consistent views. The undo segments contain the old data values that have been changed by uncommitted or recently committed transactions.

In a RAC system, users can connect with multiple instances to run database queries. Typically, users will be connected to different nodes but access the same set of data or data blocks. This situation demands that the data consistency, formerly confined to a single instance, be effectively extended to multiple instances. Therefore, buffer cache coherence from multiple instances must be maintained. Instances require three main types of concurrency:

- Concurrent reads on multiple instances – When users on two different instances need to read the same set of blocks

- Concurrent reads and writes on different instances - A user intends to read a data block that was recently modified, and the read can be for the current version of the block or for a read-consistent previous version

- Concurrent writes on different instances – When the same set of data blocks are modified by different users on different instances

Cache Coherency

Whether the database is a single-instance stand-alone system or a multi-instance RAC system, maintaining data consistency is a fundamental requirement. If data blocks are already available in the local buffer cache, then they are immediately available for user processes. Also, if they are available in another instance within the cluster, they will be transferred into the local buffer cache.

Maintaining the consistency of data blocks in the buffer caches of multiple instances is called cache coherency. The Global Cache Service (GCS), implemented by a set of Oracle processes, requires an instance to acquire cluster-wide data before a block can be modified or read. In this way, cache coherency is ensured and maintained. This resource can be explained in terms of enqueue and/or lock.

GCS synchronizes global cache access, allowing only one instance at a time to modify the block. Thus, cache coherency is maintained in the RAC system by coordinating buffer caches located on separate instances. GCS ensures that the data blocks cached in different cache buffers are maintained globally. That is why some people prefer to call cache fusion a diskless cache coherency mechanism. This is true in a sense, because the previous Oracle parallel server version (OPS) utilized forced disk writes to maintain cache coherency.

Global Cache Service

GCS is the main controlling process for cache fusion. It tracks the location and status, i.e. mode and role, of the data blocks as well as the access privileges of the various instances. GCS guarantees data integrity by employing global access levels. It maintains block modes for data blocks in the global role. It is also responsible for block transfers between instances. As shown in Figure 2.8, upon a request from an instance, GCS organizes the block shipping and the appropriate lock mode conversions. Various background processes, such as global cache service processes (LMSn) and the global enqueues service daemon (LMD), implement the global cache service.

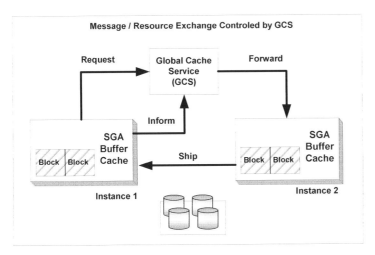

Figure 2.8: *Message/Resource Exchange Controlled by GCS*

Before going further into a detailed examination of the cache fusion mechanism and how GCS operations are performed in different scenarios, the next section will take a look at basic SGA structures and locking concepts.

SGA Components and Locking

The Oracle database is accessed through an instance. The combination of SGA (System Global Area) with one or more Oracle processes constitutes an instance. After the instance is started, the database is associated with it. This process is called database mounting. In the case of a RAC system, the database can be associated with multiple instances. The main purpose of the SGA is to store data in memory for quick access and for processing.

SGA – System Global Area

The instance is the structure or entity with which application users connect. The SGA is a group of shared memory structures that contain data and control information for the database instance. Oracle allocates memory for an SGA system whenever the instance is started. Multiple instances can be associated with a database in a RAC system, and each instance has its own SGA. The SGA contains five main areas:

- The fixed area
- The variable area
- The database buffer cache
- The log buffer
- The resource directory for a RAC system

The fixed area of the SGA contains several thousand atomic variables. These are small data structures, such as latches and pointers, which refer to other areas of the SGA. The size of the fixed area is static. It also contains general information about the state of the database and the instance which the background processes need to access.

The variable part of the SGA is made up of a large pool and a shared pool. All memory in the large pool is dynamically allocated, whereas the shared pool contains both dynamically managed memory and a permanent memory. The database buffer cache is where database block copies are held for processing. All user processes concurrently connected to the instance share access to the database buffer cache. There are many groups of buffers within the SGA.

Shared Pool and Large Pool

The shared pool segment of the SGA contains three major areas: the library cache, the dictionary cache, and buffers for parallel execution messages.

- **Library Cache** - The library cache includes the shared SQL areas, PL/SQL procedures and packages and control structures such as library cache handles, locks, synonym translations, and dependency tracking information. It contains parse trees and execution plans for shareable SQL statements, as well as pseudo code for PL/SQL program units. All users access the shared SQL areas.

- **Dictionary Cache** – Includes the usernames, segment information, profile data, tablespace information, and the sequence numbers. The dictionary cache also contains descriptive information or metadata about the schema objects. Oracle uses this metadata when parsing SQL cursors or during the compilation of PL/SQL programs.

  The dictionary cache is also known as the row cache because it holds the data in rows instead of buffers. It also holds entire blocks of data. This helps to reduce physical access to the data dictionary tables from the system tablespace and also enables fine-grained locking of individual data dictionary rows.

The large pool is an optional area. If the *large_pool_size* parameter is set, then the large pool is configured as a separate heap within a variable area of the SGA. The large pool is not a part of the shared pool.

Using the large pool instead of the shared pool decreases fragmentation of the shared pool. Unlike the shared pool, the large pool does not have an LRU list. Oracle does not attempt to age memory out of the large pool. The large pool is useful to allocate large memory allocations for:

- Session memory for the shared server and the Oracle XA interface that is used where transactions interact with more than one database

- I/O server processes

- Oracle backup and restore operations - recovery manager can use the large pool to cache I/O buffers during backup and restore operations

Redo Log Buffers

A log buffer is a circular buffer in the SGA that holds information about changes made to the database. This information is stored in the redo entries. Redo entries contain the information necessary to reconstruct or redo changes made to the database by insert, update, delete, create, alter, or drop operations. Redo entries are primarily used for database recovery as necessary.

The server processes generate redo data into the log buffer as they make changes to the data blocks in the buffer. LGWR subsequently writes entries from the redo log buffer to the online redo log.

Database Buffer Cache

The database buffer cache holds copies of data blocks read from the data files. The term data block is used to describe a block containing table data, index data, clustered data, and so on. Basically, it is a block that contains data. All user processes concurrently connected to the instance share access to the database buffer cache. The database buffer cache is logically segmented into multiple sets. This reduces contention on multiprocessor systems.

This area of the SGA contains only the buffers themselves and not their control structures. For each buffer, there is a corresponding buffer header in the variable area of the SGA.

Program Global Area (PGA)

A Program Global Area (PGA) is a memory region that contains data and control information for a server process. It is a non-shared memory region created by Oracle when a server process is started. Access to the PGA is exclusive to that server process and it is read and written only by Oracle code acting on its behalf. It contains a private SQL area and a session memory area.

A private SQL area contains data such as bind information and runtime memory structures. Each session that issues a SQL statement has a private SQL area. Session memory is the memory allocated to hold a session's variables, or logon information, and other information related to the session.

Buffer Cache Management

The database buffer cache is organized in two lists: the write list and the least-recently-used (LRU) list. The write list holds dirty buffers, which contain data that has been modified but has not yet been written to disk. The LRU list holds free buffers, pinned buffers, and dirty buffers that have not yet been moved to the write list. Free buffers do not contain any useful data and are available for use. Pinned buffers are buffers that are currently being accessed.

When an Oracle process requires data, it searches the buffer cache, finds the data blocks, and then uses the data. This is known as a cache hit. If it cannot find the data, then it must be obtained from the data file. In this case, it finds a free buffer to accommodate the data block by scanning the LRU list, starting at the least-recently-used from the end of the list. The process searches either until it finds a free buffer or until it has searched the threshold limit of buffers.

When the user process is performing a full table scan, it reads the data blocks into buffers and places them on the LRU end instead of the MRU end of the LRU list. This is because a fully scanned table is usually needed only briefly and the blocks should be moved out quickly.

Dirty Blocks

Whenever a server process changes or modifies a data block, it becomes a dirty block. Once a server process makes changes to the data block, the user may commit transactions, or transactions may not be committed for quite some time. In either case, the dirty block is not immediately written back to disk. Writing dirty blocks to disk takes place under the following two conditions:

- When a server process cannot find a clean, reusable buffer after scanning a threshold number of buffers, then the database writer process writes the dirty blocks to disk

- When the checkpoint takes place, the database writer process writes the dirty blocks to disk

Multi-Version Consistency Model

Oracle's multi-version consistency model architecture distinguishes between a current data block and one or more consistent read (CR) versions of the same block. It is important to understand the difference between the current block and the CR block. The current block contains changes for all the committed and yet-to-be-committed transactions. A consistent read (CR) block represents a consistent snapshot of the data from a previous point in time. Applying undo/rollback segment information produces consistent read versions. Thus, a single data block can reside in many buffer caches under shared resources with different versions.

Multi-version data blocks help to achieve read consistency. The read consistency model guarantees that the data block seen by a statement is consistent with respect to a single point in time and does not change during the statement execution. Readers of data do not wait for other writer's data or for other readers of the same data. At the same time, writers do not wait for other readers for the same data. Only writers wait for other writers if they attempt to write. As mentioned earlier, the undo, i.e. rollback segment provides the required information to construct the read-consistent data blocks. In case of a multi-instance system, like the RAC database, the requirement for the same data block may arise from another instance. To support this type of requirement, past images of the data blocks are created within the buffer cache. Past images will be covered later in the chapter.

Process Architecture

Oracle uses several processes to execute the different parts of Oracle code and to spawn additional processes for the users. Whenever a user connects to the database, a new server process is created on behalf of the user session. Functions of the server process include the following:

- Parse and execute SQL statements issued through the application

- Read the necessary data blocks from the disk data files into the shared database buffers of the SGA if the blocks are not already present in the SGA

- Interact and return results in such a way that the application can process the information

There are many additional processes that are automatically spawned whenever the instance starts. These processes are called background processes, and they perform the Oracle kernel functions.

Locking Mechanism

Locking is another important requirement of a multi-version consistency model. Oracle also uses a locking mechanism to control concurrent access to the data blocks. Locks help prevent destructive interaction between users accessing data blocks.

As seen earlier, when a user intends to update a data block that has already been updated by another user but is still in an uncommitted state, the update event has to wait. Without a lock mechanism, the data integrity would have been lost in this case. Locks also ensure that the data being viewed or updated by a user is not changed by other users until the user is finished using the data.

In the case of a RAC system, new and improved components or services namely, the Global Cache Service (GCS) and Global Enqueue Service (GES)) handle the lock and access management functions better than the earlier Oracle Parallel Server distributed lock manager (DLM). GES is covered in more detail later in this chapter.

RAC Components

When Oracle reads a data block into the cache, it opens a GCS resource to coordinate concurrent access by multiple instances. Oracle coordinates and converts the resource into different modes and roles, depending on the following:

- Whether the data block accessed will be modified or read
- Whether a data block exists in the cache of only one instance or in multiple caches

Thus, a resource is a concurrency control mechanism on the data blocks. It is also called a GCS resource.

In a stand-alone Oracle instance, various locks are used to control data integrity and concurrency. Similarly, the multi-instance RAC architecture deals with cached data block mode roles and the controlling access levels. The cached data blocks acquire a global nature.

GCS resources comprise the concurrency control mechanism on data blocks. They include enqueues involving the transaction locks, table locks, library cache locks, and the dictionary cache locks. Global enqueue resources are normally held for a very short time and then quickly released. For example, the TX locks are acquired whenever a transaction starts. They are released immediately after the transaction commits or rolls back. Figure 2.9 shows the main groups of resources involved in the synchronization process.

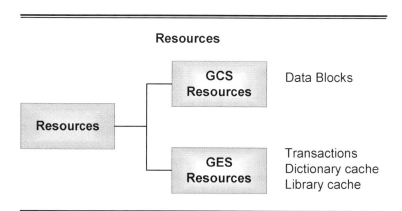

Figure 2.9: *Resources for Coordination*

Now, the three main components - the global cache service, global enqueue service, and the global resource directory - will be examined more closely.

Global Cache Service

The main function of the Global Cache Service (GCS) is to track the status and location of the data blocks. Status is the resource role and the resource mode. The GCS is the main mechanism by which cache coherency among the multiple caches is maintained.

GCS maintains the modes for blocks in the global role and is responsible for block transfers between the instances. The LMS processes handle the GCS messages and carry out the bulk of the GCS processing. GCS resource coordination is explained in detail in later sections.

Global Enqueue Service

The Global Enqueue Service (GES) tracks the status of all Oracle enqueuing mechanisms. This involves all non-cache fusion intra-instance operations. The GES performs concurrency control on dictionary cache locks, library cache locks, and transactions. It performs this operation for resources that are accessed by more than one instance.

Enqueues

What exactly is an enqueue? Enqueues are shared memory structures that serialize access to the database resources. For example, when a user updates a row and gets a row-level lock, a TX enqueue is created for that user. If another user subsequently attempts to update that same row, that user's session will block or wait on the enqueue that the initial user created. They are sometimes referred to as positive waits.

In a single instance environment, enqueues are local to the instance. With RAC, the enqueues can be global to the database. Enqueues are comprised of transaction locks, DML locks, SCN locks, and such.

Enqueues are associated with a session or a transaction. They are held longer than the latches, have finer granularity, more modes than the latches, and protect more database resources. For example, when a table lock is requested, the request is assigned to an enqueue. Oracle can use enqueues in any of three modes: null (N) mode, shared (S) mode, or exclusive (X) mode.

The GES controls access to data files and control files but not for the data blocks. GES processing includes the coordination for enqueues other than the data blocks. The resources managed by the GES include the following:

Transaction locks – It is acquired in the exclusive mode when a transaction initiates its first row level change. The lock is held until the transaction is committed or rolled back.

Library Cache locks - When a database object (such as a table, view, procedure, function, package, package body, trigger, index, cluster, or synonym) is referenced during parsing or compiling of a SQL, DML or DDL, PL/SQL, or Java statement, the process parsing or compiling the statement acquires the library cache lock in the correct mode.

Dictionary Cache Locks - Global enqueues are used in the cluster database mode. The data dictionary structure is the same for all Oracle instances in a cluster database as it is for instances in a single-instance database. However, in real application clusters, Oracle synchronizes all the dictionary caches throughout the cluster. Real application clusters use latches to do this, just as in the case of a single-instance Oracle database.

Table locks – These are the GES locks that protect the entire table(s). A transaction acquires a table lock when a table is modified. A table lock can be held in any of several modes: null (N), row share (RS), row exclusive (RX), share lock (S), share row exclusive (SRX), or exclusive (X).

Row-Level Locks

Row-level locks are the locks that protect selected rows. When a transaction updates or modifies a row, its transaction identifier is recorded in the entry as a part of the transaction list. The list is located in the header of the data block itself, and the row header is modified to point to the transaction list entry. The following statements create row-level locks:

- INSERT
- UPDATE
- DELETE
- SELECT with the FOR UPDATE clause

These row locks or row-level locks are stored in the block, and each lock refers to the global transaction lock. As in the case of a single instance, Oracle RAC controls concurrency down to the row level. The finest lock granularity is at the row level.

However, to keep the cache coherent, access to the data blocks is controlled by the GCS. This has no effect on the row-level lock. GCS resources and row locks operate independently of the GCS. An instance can request or ship the data block to another instance in the cluster without affecting the row-level locks that are held inside the data block. The row-level lock is fully controlled by the transaction that causes the row-level lock. When the transaction commits or rolls back, the row-level lock is released. In the meantime, if another transaction intends to update the same row, it has to wait until the initial transaction commits or rolls back.

The row lock method has an important advantage in maintaining data consistency, even if there are multiple instances, as in the RAC system. The behavior of the row lock and the release is the same, whether it is a single standalone database or a multi-instance RAC system. During the row lock period, even if the data block gets transferred to another instance, the row lock remains intact until released.

Global Resource Directory

The GES and GCS together maintain a Global Resource Directory (GRD) to record information about resources and enqueues. The GRD remains in memory and is stored on all the instances. Each instance manages a portion of the directory. The distributed nature of the GRD is a key point for the fault tolerance of RAC.

The GRD is an internal database that records and stores the current status of the data blocks. Whenever a block is transferred out of a local cache to another instance's cache, the GRD is updated. The following resource information is available in GRD:

- Data Block Addresses (DBA) - This is the address of the block being modified

- Location of most current version of the data block. This exists only if multiple nodes share the data block.

- Modes of the data blocks - (N)Null, (S)Shared, and (X)Exclusive

- The roles of the data blocks (local or global) - This indicates the role in which the data block is being held by the instance.

- SCN – System Change Number

- Image of the Data Block – It could be past image or current image. Current image represents the copy of the block held by the current instance. Past image represents the global dirty data block image maintained in the cache.

Resource Coordination

Since the RAC system allows many users to connect and process database SQL operations concurrently, many resources, such as data blocks and enqueues, are used simultaneously. This situation demands an effective synchronization of the concurrent tasks.

Synchronization

Within the shared cache (global cache or fused cache of multiple instances), the coordination of concurrent tasks is called synchronization. Resources such as data blocks and enqueues are synchronized as nodes within a cluster as they acquire and release ownership. The synchronization provided by real application clusters maintains a cluster wide concurrency of resources, and in turn ensures the integrity of the shared data. Even though there is seamless and transparent synchronization of concurrent tasks within the shared cache, it does not come without a cost in overhead. Processing within the local buffer cache is always faster than processing blocks across instances.

The key to successful cluster database processing is to divide the tasks that require resources among the nodes so that very little synchronization is necessary. The less synchronization necessary, the better the system's performance and scalability will be. The overhead of synchronization can be very expensive if there is excessive inter-node communication. According to Oracle studies, accessing a block within the local cache is many times faster than accessing a block in a remote cache (Figure 2.10). Accessing a block from disk is even more expensive. A combination of local cache block access with occasional access to remote cache blocks gives good performance levels.

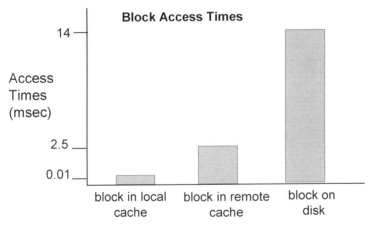

Source : Oracle World Presentation

Figure 2.10: *Block Access Times*

GCS Resource Modes and Roles

Because of data block transfers among multiple instances, the same data block can exist in multiple caches. The resource mode is defined as a concurrency control that establishes global access rights for instances in a cluster. The data block, or GCS resource, can be held in different resource modes depending on whether a resource holder intends to modify the data or read the data. The modes are as follows:

- **Null (N) mode** - Holding a resource at this level conveys that there are no access rights. Null mode is usually held as a placeholder, even if the resource is not actively used.

- **Shared (S) mode** - When a resource is held at this level, it will ensure that the data block is not modified by another session but will allow concurrent shared access.

- **Exclusive (X) mode** - This level grants the holding process exclusive access. Other processes cannot write to the resource. It may have consistent read blocks.

The resource mode is an important mechanism to maintain data integrity and avoid data corruption issues. GCS resources are specified to have global roles or local roles. These roles are mutually exclusive.

- When a block is first read into the cache of an instance and other instances have not read the same block, then the block is said to be locally managed and is therefore assigned a local role.

- After the block has been modified by the local instance and transmitted to another instance, it is considered to be globally managed, and is therefore assigned a global role.

Basically, the concept of role supplements the access mode characteristic. A typical data block has both of these characteristics.

Concept of Past Image

The past image concept was introduced in the RAC version of Oracle 9i to maintain data integrity. In an Oracle database, a typical data block is not written to the disk immediately, even after it is dirtied. When the same dirty data block is requested by another instance for write or read purposes, an image of the block is created at the owning instance, and only that block is shipped to the requesting instance. This backup image of the block is called the past image (PI) and is kept in memory. In the event of failure, Oracle can reconstruct the current version of the block by reading PIs. It is also possible to have more than one past image in the memory depending on how many times the data block was requested in the dirty stage.

A past image copy of the data block is different from a CR block, which is needed for reconstructing a read-consistent image. A CR version of a block represents a consistent snapshot of the data at a point in time. It is constructed by applying information from the undo/rollback segments. The PI image copy helps the recovery process and aids in maintaining data integrity.

For example, suppose user A of Instance 1 has updated row 2 on block 5. Later, user B of Instance 2 intends to update row 6 on the same block 5. The GCS transfers block 5 from Instance A to Instance B. At this point, the past image (PI) for block 5 is created on Instance A.

Lock Modes

From the examination of resource roles, resource modes, and past images, the next step is to consider the possible resource access modes as shown in Table 2.2.

There are three characters that distinguish lock or block access modes. The first letter represents the lock mode, the second character represents the lock role, and the third character (a number) indicates any past images for the lock in the local instance.

LOCK MODE	DESCRIPTION
NL0	Null Local and No past images
SL0	Shared Local with no past image
XL0	Exclusive Local with no past image

LOCK MODE	DESCRIPTION
NG0	Null Global – Instance owns current block image
SG0	Global Shared Lock – Instance owns current image
XG0	Global Exclusive Lock – Instance own current image
NG1	Global Null – Instance owns the past image block
SG1	Shared Global – Instance owns past image
XG1	Global Exclusive Lock – Instance owns past image.

Table 2.2: *Lock Modes*

When a block is brought into the local cache of an instance, it is acquired with the local role. But if a dirty buffer for the same data block is present in a remote instance, a past image is created in the remote instance before the data block is sent to the requesting instance's cache. Therefore, the data block resource acquires a global role.

For recovery purposes, instances that have past images will keep those past images in their buffer cache until the master instance prompts the lock to release them. When the buffers are discarded, the instance holding the past image will write a block written redo (BWR) to the redo stream. The BWR indicates that the block has already been written to disk and is not needed for recovery by the instance. Buffers are discarded when the disk write is initiated on the master instance. The master instance is where the current status and position of the data block is maintained.

This has been a review of how a GCS resource maintains its access mode and its role. There is another feature called the buffer state, which is covered in the next section.

Block Access Modes and Buffer States

The buffer state indicates the status of a buffer in the local cache of an instance. Information about the buffer state can be seen in the dynamic performance view *v$bh*. The buffer state of a block relates to the access mode of the block. For example, if a buffer state is in exclusive current

(XCUR) state, it indicates that the instance owns the resource in exclusive mode.

To see a buffer's state, query the STATUS column of the *v$bh* dynamic performance view. The *v$bh* view provides information about the block access mode and their buffer state names as follows:

- **Buffer state 'CR'** - indicates that the block access mode is N (null). It means the owning instance can perform a consistent read of the block, if the instance holds an older version of the data.

- **Buffer state 'SCUR'** - indicates that the block access mode is S (shared). It means the instance has shared access to the block and can only perform reads.

- **Buffer state 'XCUR'** - indicates that access mode is X (exclusive). It means the instance has exclusive access to the block and can modify it.

- **Buffer state 'PI'** - indicates that block access mode is N (null). It means that the instance has made changes to the block but retains copies of past images.

BLOCK ACCESS MODE	BUFFER STATE NAME	DESCRIPTION
X	XCUR	Instance has exclusive access to the block and therefore can modify the block
S	SCUR	Instance has shared access to the block and can only perform reads
NULL	CR	Contains an older version of the data. Can perform consistent read
--	PI	Past Image Exist (useful for recovery)

Table 2.3: *Buffer States Shown in v$bh View*

Only the SCUR and PI buffer states are real application cluster-specific. There can be only one copy of any block buffered in the XCUR state at any time. To perform modifications on a block, a process must assign an XCUR buffer state to the buffer containing the data block.

For example, if another instance requests a read access to the most current version of the same block, then Oracle changes the access mode from exclusive to shared, sends the current read version of the block to the requesting instance, and keeps a PI buffer if the buffer contained a dirty block

At this point, the first instance has the current block and the requesting instance also has the current block in shared mode. Therefore, the role of the resource becomes global. There can be multiple shared current (SCUR) versions of this block cached throughout the cluster database at any given point of time.

Cache Fusion Scenarios

The GCS plays a key role in performing the necessary block transfers. Three scenarios are presented to explain the concept of cache fusion:

- Scenario 1 - Read/Read
- Scenario 2 - Write/Write
- Scenario 3 - Disk Write

Scenario 1: Read/Read

Figure 2.11 shows Scenario 1, where a typical data block is requested from another instance where it is in shared access mode with a local role. Instance 1 desires to read a data block and it makes a request to the GCS, which keeps track of the resources, location, and status. The GCS in turn forwards the request to owning Instance 2.

A) Read / Read Cache Fusion - GCS processing

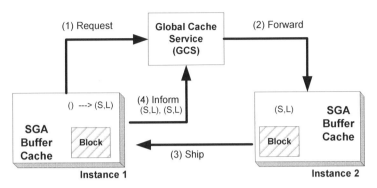

Figure 2.11: *Read/Read Cache Fusion – GCS Processing*

The holding instance (Instance 2) transmits a copy of the block to the requesting instance (Instance 1), but keeps the resource in shared mode and also retains the local role.

Instance 2 now informs the GCS of its own resource disposition (S, L) and also that of the instance that sent the block (S, L). Thus, there is no disk read involved. The block transfer took place through the high-speed private interconnect.

Scenario 2: Write/Write

As shown in Figure 2.12, instance 1 intends to modify or update the data block and submits a request to GCS. The GCS transmits the request on to the holder (Instance 2).

Upon receiving the message, Instance 2 sends the block to Instance 1. Before sending the block, the resource is downgraded to null mode and the changed (dirty) buffer is kept as a PI. Thus, the role changes to global (G) because the block is dirty.

Along with the block, Instance 2 informs the requestor that it retained a PI copy and a null resource. The same message also specifies that the requestor can take the block held in exclusive mode and with a global role (X, G).

B) Write / Write Cache Fusion - GCS processing

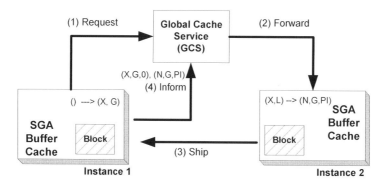

Figure 2.12: *Write/Write Cache Fusion — GCS Processing*

Upon receipt of the block and the resource dispositions, Instance 1 informs the GCS of the mode and role (X, G). Note that the data block is not written to disk before the resource is granted to the other instance. That is, DBWR is not involved in the cache coherency scheme at this stage.

Scenario 3: Disk Write

As shown in Figure 2.13, Instance 2 first sends a write request to the GCS. This might be due to a user-executing checkpoint on Instance 2. Note that there is a past image for the block on Instance 2. The GCS forwards the request to Instance 1 (the current block holder). The GCS remembers that a write at the system change number (SCN) is pending and it also remembers that it has to notify the nodes that have PIs of the same block.

Instance 1 then receives the write request and writes the block to disk. Instance 1 completes the write and notifies the GCS. Instance 1 also informs the GCS that the resource role can become local because the instance has completed the write of the current block. After completion of the protocol, all PIs of the block should be discarded.

C) Write blocks to disk - GCS Processing

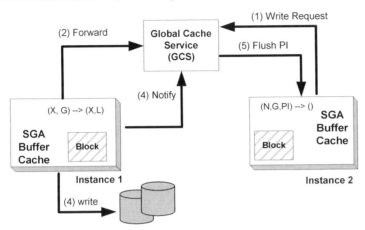

Figure 2.13: *Write Blocks to Disk – GCS Processing*

Upon receipt of the notification, the GCS orders all PI holders to discard, or flush, their PIs. Discarding, in this case, means that upon receipt of the message the PI holder records that the current block has been written and the buffer is released. The PI is no longer needed for recovery. The buffer is essentially free and the resource previously held in null mode is closed.

Block Transfers Using Cache Fusion – Example

The following is another example of how block shipping takes place. Assume that in a 3-node RAC cluster a typical block (of table 'salesman') is brought into Instance 3 by a select operation of user C. Initially, the instance acquires SL0 (shared lock with no past image) and the same Block/Lock-element undergoes many conversions as different users at different instances handle it. The following operations show a clear movement of the blocks among the instances using cache fusion. It also shows the complexity involved. Refer to Figures 2.14 and 2.15.

In Stage (1), the data block is read into the buffer of Instance 3 and it opens with an SL0 mode (Shared Local without any past image):

```
select sales_rank from salesman where salesid = 10;
```

This gives a value of 30. Thus, the data block is protected by a resource in shared mode (S) and its role is local (L). This indicates that the block only exists in the local cache of Instance 3.

A) Data Block shipping using Cache Fusion

Instance 1	Instance 2	Instance 3	
Stage (1)			
Lock held : none -------------	Lock held : none -------------	Lock held : SL0 ------------- Shared Local No Past Image	Select on Insta-3
Stage (2)			
Lock held : none -------------	Lock held : SL0 ------------- Shared Local No Past Image	Lock held : SL0 ------------- Shared Local No Past Image	Select on Insta-2 Block shipped from insta-3 to inst-2
Stage (3)			
Lock held : none -------------	Lock held : XL0 ------------- Excl Local No Past Image	Lock held : none -------------	Update on Insta-2 Lock drop at inst-3
Stage (4)			
Lock held : XG0 ------------- Excl Global No Past Image	Lock held : NG1 ------------- Null Global with Past Image	Lock held : none -------------	Update on Inst-1 Block Shipping to Inst-1 Downgrade at Inst-2

Figure 2.14: *Data Block Shipping using Cache Fusion*

In Stage (2), user B issues the same select statement against the salesman table. Instance 2 will need the same block; therefore, the block is shipped from Instance 3 to Instance 2 via the cache fusion interconnect. There is no disk read at this time. Both instances are in shared (S) mode and the role is local (L). So far, no buffer is dirtied.

In Stage (3), user B decides to update the row and commit at Instance 2. The new sales rank is 24. At this stage, Instance 2 acquires XL0 (Exclusive Local) at Instance 2 and the share lock is removed on Instance 3.

```
Update salesman set sales_rank = 24
Where salesid = 10;
```

In Stage (4), user A decides to update on Instance 1 the same row, and therefore the block, with the sales rank value of 40. It finds that the block is dirty in Instance 2. Therefore, the data block is shipped to Instance 1 from Instance 2; however, a past image of the data block is created on Instance 2 and the lock mode is also converted to Null with a global role. Instance 2 now has a NG1 (Null Global with past image). At this time, Instance 1 will have exclusive lock with global role (XG0).

In Stage (5), user C executes a select on Instance 3 on the same row. The data block from Instance 1 being the most recent copy, it is shipped to Instance 3. As a result, the lock on Instance 1 is converted to shared global with past image (SG1). On the requesting instance (Instance 1), the SG0 lock resource is created.

```
Select sales_rank from salesman
Where salesid = 10;
```

B) Data Block shipping using Cache Fusion

Instance 1	Instance 2	Instance 3	
Stage (5)			
Lock held : SG1 ------------- Share Global with Past Image	Lock held : NG1 ------------- Null Global with Past Image	Lock held : SG0 ------------- Share Global No Past Image	Select on Inst-3 Shipping to Inst-3 from Inst-1 Downgrade at Inst-1
Stage (6)			
Lock held : SG1 ------------- Share Global with Past Image	Lock held : SG1 ------------- Share Global with Past Image	Lock held : SG0 ------------- Share Global No past Image	Select on Inst-2 Shipping to Inst-2 from Inst-1 Downgrade at Inst-1
Stage (7)			
Lock held : NG1 ------------- Null Global with Past Image	Lock held : NG1 ------------- Null Global with Past Image	Lock held : XG0 ------------- Exclu. Global No Past Image	Update on Inst-3 Downgrade at Inst-1 and Inst-2
Stage (8)			
Lock held : none -------------	Lock held : none -------------	Lock held : XL0 ------------- Exclu. Local No Past Image	Checkpipoint at Inst-3 Becomes Local Insta-2 and Insta-1 discard past images.

Figure 2.15: *Data Block Shipping Using Cache Fusion*

In Stage (6), user B issues the same select against the salesman table on Instance 2. Instance 2 will request a consistent read copy of the buffer from another instance, which happens to be the current master.

Therefore, Instance 1 will ship the block to Instance 2, where it will be acquired with SG1. Then, at Instance 1, the lock will be converted to SG1.

In Stage (7), user C on Instance C updates the same row. Therefore, Instance 3 acquires an exclusive lock and Instances 1 and 2 will be downgraded to NG1 (Null global with past image). Instance 3 will have exclusive mode with a global role.

In Stage (8), the checkpoint is initiated and a write to disk takes place at Instance 3. Instance 1 and Instance 2 will discard their past images. At Instance 3, the lock mode will become exclusive with a local role.

The stages above illustrate that consistency is maintained even though the same block is requested at different levels. These operations are transparent to the application. All the mode and role conversions are handled by Oracle without any human configuration.

If there are considerable cross-instance updates and queries for the same set of blocks, blocks are moved across without resorting to disk read or disk writes. However, there will be considerable lock conversions, which may be expensive, though they are less expensive than disk read/writes.

Block Access, Grants, and Interrupts

The GCS maintains the status of the resources. It also keeps an inventory of the access requests for the data blocks. After the blocks are transferred from one instance to another to meet requests, the requesting processes need to be notified that the block is actually available. Therefore, processes utilize interrupts to inform of the arrival or completion of block transfers. The GCS uses various interrupts to manage resource allocation. These interrupts are:

- **Blocking Interrupt** - When exclusive access is needed for a requestor, the GCS sends a blocking interrupt to a process that currently owns the shared resource, notifying it that a request for an exclusive resource is waiting

- **Acquisition Interrupt** - When the requested access (e.g., exclusive) is made available after releasing an earlier access mode, an acquisition interrupt is sent to alert the process that has requested the exclusive resource. The acquisition interrupt helps to notify the requesting process.

- **Block Arrival Interrupt** - When a process requests a block from the GCS, the request is forwarded to the instance holding the block. Then the requested block is sent to the requesting process, and the process informs the GCS that it has received the block. This notification is called block arrival interrupt.

The block requests are granted for many processes at the same time, but they follow a queuing mechanism. The GCS maintains two types of queues for resource requests. If the GCS is unable to grant a resource request immediately, then the GCS puts it in the convert queue. The GCS then tracks all waiting requests. Once a resource is granted to the requesting process, it is kept in the granted queue. The GCS tracks resource requests in the granted queue.

Cache Fusion and Recovery

In the RAC system, whenever there is a node failure, the instance running on the failed node crashes and becomes unusable. There can be several reasons for such a failure. In this section, focus will be placed on the changes that take place in the global cache and how the recovery of the failed instance is undertaken by one of the surviving instances.

Recovery Features

Only the cache resources that reside on the failed nodes or are mastered by the GCS on the failed nodes need to be rebuilt or re-mastered. Rebuilt or re-master does not mean building a block; the lock ownership is merely changed and this is explained later with examples.

All resources previously mastered at the failed instance are redistributed across the remaining instances. These resources are reconstructed at their new master instance. All other resources previously mastered at surviving instances remain unaffected.

The cluster manager first detects the node and instance failure. It communicates the failure status to the GCS by way of the LMON process. At this stage, any surviving instance in the cluster initiates the recovery process.

Remember, instance recovery does not include restarting the failed instance or recovering applications that were running on that instance. Also note that, even after a node failure and instance loss, the redo log file of the failed instance is still available to the other recovering instance since the redo log file is located on the shared cluster file system or shared raw partition. This is an important feature of the RAC system.

Because of past images, instance recovery is performed differently in the RAC implementation. The SMON process of a surviving instance performs recovery of the failed instance or thread. However, note that the foreground process performs recovery in a stand-alone instance.

Recovery Methodology and Steps

Oracle performs the following steps to recover:

1. In the initial phase of recovery, GES enqueues are reconfigured and the global resource directory is frozen. All GCS resource requests and writes are temporarily halted.

2. GCS resources are reconfigured among the surviving instances. One of the surviving instances becomes the recovering instance. The SMON process of the recovering instance starts a first pass of the redo log read of the failed instance's redo thread.

3. Block resources that need to be recovered are identified and the global resource directory is reconstructed. Pending requests or writes are cancelled or replayed.

4. Resources identified in the previous log read phase are defined as recovery resources. Buffer space for recovery is allocated.

5. Assuming that there are past images of blocks to be recovered in other caches in the cluster, source buffers are requested from other instances. The resource buffers are the starting point of recovery for a particular block.

6. All resources and enqueues required for subsequent processing have been acquired and the global resource directory is now unfrozen.

Any data blocks that are not in recovery can now be accessed. At this time, the system is partially available.

7. The SMON merges the redo thread order by SCN to ensure that changes are written in an orderly fashion. This process is important for multiple simultaneous failures. If multiple instances die simultaneously, neither the PI buffers nor the current buffers for a data block can be found in any surviving instance's cache. Then a log merger of the failed instances is performed.

8. Now the second pass of recovery begins and redo is applied to data files, releasing the recovery resources immediately after block recovery, so that more and more blocks become available as cache recovery proceeds.

9. After all blocks have been recovered and recovery resources have been released, the system is available for normal use.

Figure 2.16 shows the basic steps in the recovery.

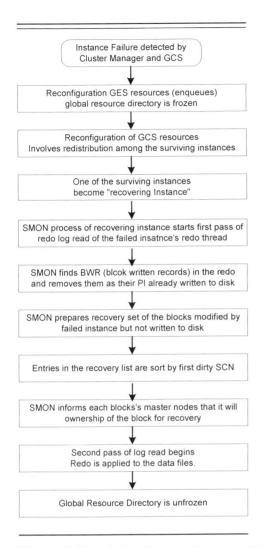

Figure 2.16: *Online Instance Recovery Steps*

Recovery Process – Re-mastering Resources

The recovery process is done in two passes. The first pass will construct recovery sets and the appropriate lock modes after eliminating the not-needed entries like BWR. This process makes use of extra buffers in the recovering instance's cache to store the recovery list. In the second pass, the actual recovery of the blocks takes place, and redo is applied to the data files.

The following is an examination of some of these situations to facilitate understanding of how the process works. The scenario involves a RAC with three instances (A, B, C) and instance C has failed. Instance A has taken over the role of recovering instance and Instance B is an open, good instance. The situation is constructed as if the failed instance existed.

Scenario 1:

Neither the recovering instance (A) nor the open instance (B) has a lock element or it may be in NL0 mode. This indicates that the failed instance had XL0. Therefore, SMON acquires a lock in XL0 mode, reads the block from disk, and applies redo changes. Thusly, the block is kept in the recovery set. Later, DBWR writes the recovery buffer out when recovery is completed.

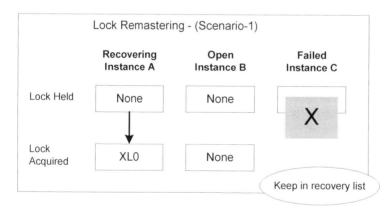

Figure 2.17: *Lock Re-Mastering – (Scenario-1)*

Scenario 2:

Instance B has the block buffer in either XL0 mode or SL0, but the recovering instance (A) does not have anything. Since Instance B is holding the lock in exclusive local mode, it is more current than the redo stream. Therefore, no recovery is needed. There is also no need to write this block to disk.

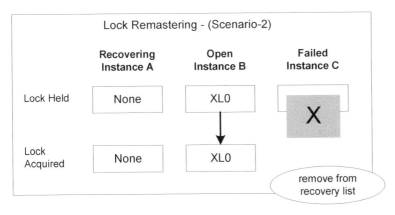

Figure 2.18: *Lock Remastering – (Scenario-2)*

Scenario 3:

Instance B has the block buffer in either XG# mode or SG# mode (both global), but the recovering instance (A) does not have anything. Here, the resource is in global role. Therefore, SMON initiates the write of the current block on Instance B. No recovery is needed because a current copy of the block exists in Instance B. The entry is removed from the recovery set. Write completion will release the recovery buffer and Instance A acquires NG1.

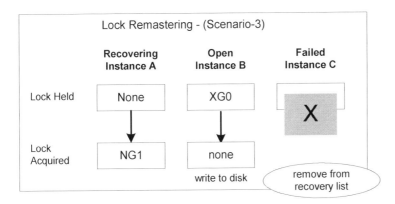

Figure 2.19: *Lock Remastering – (Scenario-3)*

Scenario 4:

The recovering instance (A) does not have anything and Instance B has NG1 mode, which indicates the failed instance had the more current block, perhaps something like XG0. Therefore, Instance A gets a consistent-read image block based on SCN from Instance B, and acquires XG0 mode. It keeps the block in the recovery list.

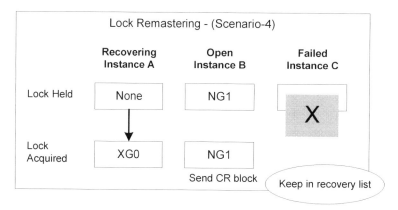

Figure 2.20: *Lock Re-Mastering – (Scenario-4)*

Scenario 5:

The recovering instance (A) has the lock element in SL0 or XL0 (both local) and other instances have no lock elements on this block. This scenario requires no recovery as the current copy of the buffer is present in Instance A. It removes the redo entry from the recovery list.

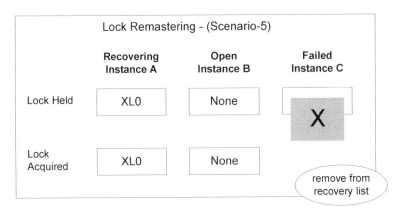

Figure 2.21: *Lock Re-mastering – (Scenario-5)*

Scenario 6:

The recovering instance (A) has the lock element in SG# or XG# (both Global). Since it has a global role, shared or exclusive, the status on the other open instance is immaterial. Therefore, Instance A initiates the writing of the current block to disk. There is no recovery needed and it releases the buffer from the redo list.

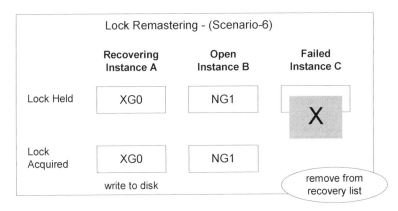

Figure 2.22: *Lock Remastering – (Scenario-6)*

Scenario 7:

Instance A has the lock element in NG1 and Instance B has XG# or SG#. This involves writing the current block on Instance B and no recovery is needed.

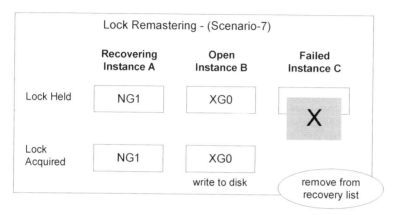

Figure 2.23: *Lock Remastering – (Scenario-7)*

Scenario 8:

Instance A has the lock element in NG1 and Instance B has the lock in NG0/NG1 mode. It indicates the failed instance was holding the resource in exclusive mode. This involves getting a consistent-read copy from the highest past image, based on SCN, and applying redo changes. Instance B sends the CR block to Instance A. This block is kept for recovery.

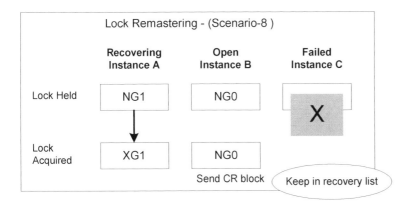

Figure 2.24: *Lock Remastering – (Scenario-8)*

Thus, after the first pass, the recovering instance will have locks on every block in the recovery list (set). Other instances will not be able to acquire these locks until the recovery operation is completed. Now the second pass begins, the redo is applied to the data files.

During instance recovery, if the recovering instance dies, a surviving instance, if one exists, will acquire instance recovery enqueue and starts recovery. If a non-recovering instance fails, SMON will abort recovery, release the IR enqueue, and the next live instance will reattempt instance recovery.

Conclusion

In this chapter, topics concerning Oracle RAC Architecture have been covered. All the components that make up Oracle 11g RAC were reviewed. Memory Structures, background processes, cluster ready services, and physical and logical structures of the database dispatchers have been examined. The differences between the database instance and database have been identified. The concept of thread was explored and how it is extended in case of RAC database system.

This chapter has also explained the nature of cache fusion, resource coordination, cache-to-cache transfers, resource management, and lock conversions. It also covered instance failure and the associated re-mastering of resources by the surviving instance.

References

Source Metalink.com
Oracle.com
Pro Oracle Database 10g on Linux

Jeff Hunter's install guide.
http://www.idevelopment.info/data/Oracle/DBA_tips/Oracle11gRAC/CLUSTER_10.shtml

Tim Hall's install guide
http://www.oracle-base.com/articles/11g/OracleDB11gR1RACInstallationOnLinuxUsingNFS.php

Storage and RAC

There are many options for data storage in a RAC environment. This chapter will explore some of those options. It is important for the DBA and System Administrator to work together to examine the system and determine the optimal environment for the RAC cluster.

RAC Using Raw Storage

Some Oracle files can be written to unformatted disk areas known as raw devices. Some sources may also call these raw volumes, raw partitions, or raw disks. The Oracle files which can be written to raw devices are:

- OCR
- Voting disk
- Datafiles
- Redo logs
- Control file
- SPFILE

It is worth noting that the archive logs and RMAN backups do not make the raw storage list. This is because a raw device can only handle one file at a time. Given a partition with no filesystem, there are three available options: format the partition for a particular filesystem, use the partition in an ASM diskgroup, or use the partition as a raw device on which a single file may be placed.

One reason behind the popularity of raw devices is performance. In the past, raw devices were the only way by which a system could be set up to

---

take advantage of Direct I/O (DIO); that is, I/O that bypasses the filesystem cache. In fact, Direct I/O has been supported in the ext3 filesystem since Enterprise Linux 2.1. Support for enhanced Asynchronous I/O (AIO) with Direct I/O was added in Enterprise Linux 4, even when using an ext-based filesystem. According to Red Hat, ext3 filesystem access with AIO and DIO can perform within 3% of raw I/O performance. Direct I/O is also enabled when using OCFS/OCFS2.

> 🔔 The *filesystemio_options* parameter allows a DBA to direct how Oracle will perform I/O. A setting of 'directio' will allow Direct I/O access. 'asynch' allows Asynchronous I/O access. 'setall' allows both. Consult the OS specific documentation to determine if the system is optimized for both DIO and AIO.

In Oracle 11g it is very common to find the OCR and voting disk of a RAC cluster on raw devices. This is because those two files are very small, very static in size, and cannot be placed in ASM. However, according to Oracle Metalink (Oracle's support system), raw device support will be completely unavailable in Oracle 12g. This may be due to the fact that raw devices have been declared obsolete in Linux since kernel version 2.6.3, and support for raw devices will soon be gone. However, there is no need to fear this change. Instead, it is only necessary to make room for a few changes in vocabulary.

Those familiar with using raw devices on Linux may get a shock when using Redhat Enterprise Linux 5 (RHEL5) or Oracle Enterprise Linux 5 (OEL5) as there appears to be no raw device support. As mentioned above, in kernel version 2.6.3, this support is officially deprecated. However, it is still possible to configure a */dev/raw* volume using udev rules.

In RHEL4 it was possible to simply place entries in */etc/sysconfig/rawdevices* which mapped a block device, i.e. */dev/sda1*, to a raw device, i.e. */dev/raw1*. Using the raw devices service, the mapping would take effect and */dev/raw* would be a usable area.

> 🔔 In a Windows environment, a raw device is simply a logical partition created in Disk Manager that is not formatted and has no drive letter.

In RHEL and OEL 5, entries must be made under the rules specified in */etc/udev*. Udev is responsible for managing the */dev* area in Linux, and udev rules determine how */dev* will be presented.

While */bin/raw* can be used to bind a block device to a raw device, */bin/raw* binding alone is not meant to be a long-term configuration. One of the primary purposes of udev is to keep disk areas and naming consistent.

To create a udev rule that maps block device */dev/sda1* to raw device */dev/raw1*:

1. Create a file called: */etc/udev/rules.d/60-raw.rules*

   ▪ Any number greater than or equal to 60 may be used

2. Add the line: *ACTION=="add"*, *"KERNEL=="sda1"*, *RUN+="/bin/raw /dev/raw/raw1 %N"*

   Despite this ability, in Oracle 11g there is really no point in creating */dev/raw* devices unless it is being done for comfort value. This is because in Oracle 10.2.0.2 up, block devices are accessible by Oracle using the O_DIRECT flag, meaning they are able to perform direct I/O without using the rawio interface. OUI and ASMlib will both accept a block device (i.e. */dev/sda1*) as input for file placement in Oracle 11g on Linux.

> 🔔 In 10gR2, even though Oracle allowed block devices to be used in 10.2.0.2 and up, OUI was not able to handle a block device name. Instead, symbolic links had to be created to map the block device to a different name under /dev. While effective, this does not follow the udev rules.

Even with direct support for block devices, in order to configure a block device for Oracle's use, udev rules must still be created. Since

---

RAC Using Raw Storage

udev manages the */dev* area, the rules will need to state ownership of the block devices in order to grant Oracle the permissions necessary to use them.

3. Edit the file: */etc/udev/rules.d/50-udev.rules*

4. At the bottom of the file, add the new rules in the following format:

```
KERNEL=="blockdevicename", OWNER="deviceowner", GROUP="devicegroup",
MODE="4digitpermissions"
```

- **Block device name** - the name of the block device. For instance, if the device is listed as */dev/sda1*, the block device name is sda1.

- **Device owner** - should be set to the name of the OS user that will own the block device. For instance, if the device is going to be used for placement of the OCR, root should be the owner. For the voting disk or ASM disks, oracle should be the owner.

- **Device group** - should be set to the name of the group which owns the block device. This will usually be oinstall or dba.

- **4digitpermissions** - should be set to the permissions mask of the block device. For the OCR and ASM devices this will be 0640. For the voting disk, it will usually be 0644.

It is important to note that even though Oracle is writing to a block device instead of a raw device, this is still technically raw storage. Instead of using the rawio interface, a direct interface to the block device has been provided by the Linux kernel and Oracle.

The limitations of raw are still a factor when writing to block devices. Only one file may be present on any single block device when the device is unformatted.

Creating the OCR and voting disk on block devices is a popular option, as the only other storage method available is a cluster file system such as OCFS2 which presents yet another layer of dependency for an Oracle installation. For datafiles, control files, SPFILEs, redo logs, RMAN backups, and archive logs, ASM is the new de facto standard for RAC storage.

RAC Using Automatic Storage Management (ASM)

ASM was introduced in Oracle 10g and is widely used in both RAC and single instance environments. Oracle created ASM as a way for DBAs to simplify their storage options, especially when using a cluster environment.

ASM will work directly with block devices and act as a combination volume manager and filesystem specifically built for Oracle files. However, the ASM filesystem is not available to the operating system without the use of special tools.

This means that ASM volumes, called diskgroups, cannot simply be mounted at the OS level and browsed, copied, edited, or otherwise managed. However, a whole host of commands have been created which can be performed through SQL*Plus. In addition, tools such as ASMlib and ASMCMD simplify management of files inside of ASM volumes.

Also, ASM gives storage administrators and DBAs the option to add or remove disks from the configuration as needed, allowing easy scalability at the storage level. This level of granularity was previously not possible with most Logical Volume Managers (LVMs).

Block devices at the OS level are recognized by ASM as disks. Even if a block device is formed of a twelve-disk RAID 10 volume, in ASM it is still considered a disk. Disks can then be added to ASM diskgroups, which take on the format +NAME. The plus sign (+) is used in naming an ASM diskgroup and when creating files inside of an ASM diskgroup.

When multiple disks are added to an ASM diskgroup, ASM will automatically stripe data between the disks in the diskgroup. For instance, if a shelf of 14 disks is made into a single RAID 10 LUN (7 mirrored disks striped), and another four disks are made into a RAID 10 LUN, it would be possible to combine the two into an ASM diskgroup.

ASM will balance the data as evenly as possible between the two disks (in reality, volumes). This is done to optimize I/O throughput.

Disks can be added to an ASM diskgroup in a variety of ways depending on the operating system. As discussed in the previous section, raw volumes will become unsupported in Oracle 12g. However, the same block device support that works with the OCR and the voting disk applies to ASM as well.

Linux - ASMlib

On Linux, a package called ASMlib allows quick and easy disk detection and stamping. Using the tool, a DBA can scan the system for available disks, stamp the disks as ASM usable, and share discovery across multiple nodes of a RAC cluster.

To install ASMlib, navigate to:
http://www.oracle.com/technology/tech/linux/asmlib/index.html

The compiled packages are available for download on Redhat Enterprise Linux (RHEL), SUSE, and Oracle Enterprise Linux (OEL). The source code can also be downloaded from http://oss.oracle.com under the GNU Public License (GPL).

To install and configure ASMlib, three packages are required:

- oracleasm-support
- oracleasm-lib
- oracleasm

Note: The support and library packages are at version 2.0 as of the time of this writing, which is supported across all kernel releases. However, the oracleasm package must be version 1.0 for Linux 2.4, and 2.0 for Linux 2.6.

Once the packages are downloaded, they must be installed by root via rpm.

```
rpm -Uvh oracleasm-support-2.0.0-1.i386.rpm /
   oracleasm-lib-2.0.0-1.i386.rpm /
   oracleasm-2.6.9-5.0.5-ELsmp-2.0.0-1.i686.rpm
```

After the installation, the ASMlib software will be installed, as will a management script called */etc/init.d/oracleasm*. Using this script, ASM disks can be found, stamped, and scanned. In order to set up ASMlib initially, the following command must be run as root:

```
/etc/init.d/oracleasm configure
```

This command configures bootup options for ASM in order to ensure that ASM disks are loaded before Oracle's software attempts to utilize the disks.

```
[root@ractest /]# /etc/init.d/oracleasm configure
Configuring the Oracle ASM library driver.

This will configure the on-boot properties of the Oracle ASM library
driver.  The following questions will determine whether the driver is
loaded on boot and what permissions it will have.  The current values
will be shown in brackets ('[]').  Hitting  without typing an
answer will keep that current value.  Ctrl-C will abort.

Default user to own the driver interface []: oracle
Default group to own the driver interface []: dba
Start Oracle ASM library driver on boot (y/n) [n]: y
Fix permissions of Oracle ASM disks on boot (y/n) [y]: y
Writing Oracle ASM library driver configuration        [   OK   ]
Creating /dev/oracleasm mount point                    [   OK   ]
Loading module "oracleasm"                             [   OK   ]
Mounting ASMlib driver filesystem                      [   OK   ]
Scanning system for ASM disks                          [   OK   ]
```

Figure 3.1: *Configuring ASMlib*

 Even though this is being run as root, it is recommended that one choose the oracle user a dba group to be the owners of the driver interface during the configuration.

It is also worth mentioning that the options chosen for automatic startup and shutdown are not permanent. These options can be changed using the */etc/init.d/oracleasm* script with the enable and disable arguments.

Once ASMlib is completely configured, the root user can apply the */etc/init.d/oracleasm* script to create new ASM disks using block devices. Other nodes in the cluster can then scan for these disks and become aware of them. In order to label disks as ASM disks, the following command can be used:

```
/etc/init.d/oracleasm createdisk DISKNAME /dev/path
```

- **DISKNAME** - The ASM label for the disk. The name chosen does not matter, but it is a good idea to choose names logically that will help with management down the road.

- **/dev/path** - The path to the block device to be labeled. For instance, */dev/sdb1* is a block device that ASM could label for its own use.

```
[root@ractest /]# /etc/init.d/oracleasm createdisk DATA1 /dev/sdb1
Creating Oracle ASM disk "DATA1"                    [  OK  ]
[root@ractest /]# /etc/init.d/oracleasm createdisk DATA2 /dev/sdb2
Creating Oracle ASM disk "DATA2"                    [  OK  ]
[root@ractest /]# /etc/init.d/oracleasm createdisk DATA3 /dev/sdb3
Creating Oracle ASM disk "DATA3"                    [  OK  ]
[root@ractest /]#
```

Figure 3.2: *Creating ASM Disks with Oracleasm*

After the disks have been created, verify the disk labels with the *listdisks* parameter:

```
# /etc/init.d/oracleasm listdisks
DATA1
DATA2
DATA3
```

It is a good idea to get sysadmins used to the idea of querying disks to make sure they are not being used for ASM before performing any possibly harmful actions against the system's disks. The *querydisk* argument can be used for this purpose:

```
/etc/init.d/oracleasm querydisk /dev/path
```

- **/dev/path** - A block device to query for the presence of an ASM label.

```
[root@ractest /]# /etc/init.d/oracleasm querydisk /dev/sdb1
Checking if device "/dev/sdb1" is an Oracle ASM disk         [  OK  ]
```

Figure 3.3: *Querying Disks with Oracleasm*

If the queried device is not an ASM disk, then FAILED will be displayed between the brackets.

In a RAC configuration, all nodes must be able to see the same ASM devices. The good news is that one does not have to go through the creation of disks with ASMlib on each system in the RAC cluster. However, one must install ASMlib on each node.

Once disks have been created on one node, the other nodes can be updated using the */etc/init.d/oracleasm* scandisks function. Using the *scandisks* argument will instruct oracleasm to browse the */dev* tree to find devices which have been labeled for use by ASMlib.

```
[root@ractest2 /]# /etc/init.d/oracleasm scandisks
Scanning system for ASM disks                               [  OK  ]
```

Figure 3.4: *Scanning Disks on Other Nodes with Oracleasm*

 Even though disks have been tagged as being ASM disks, one must still add the disks into an ASM diskgroup as described in an upcoming section.

Windows

On Windows, ASM disks will incorporate logical drives set up using the Windows Disk Management tool (Start → All Programs →

Administrative Tools → Computer Management). These drives should contain no filesystem and should not be assigned a drive letter.

ASM can be configured during the installation of Oracle 11g or later through DBCA. In Windows, the Stamp Disks button allows the DBA to select logical drives that should be used for ASM. Much like ASMlib, disks that are available as candidate devices can be labeled as ASM drives.

> 🔔 While stamping disks, one may notice the OCR and voting disks in the list. These disks will have a status of "Oracle raw device file" while available disks will say "Candidate device."

Once disks have been stamped as ASM candidates, it will be possible to add them to an ASM diskgroup. All disks will have a prefix of \\.\ORCLDISK plus any prefix added while stamping. For instance, during labeling, if the DBA elects to use a prefix of FLASH, labeled disks will take the format \\.\ORCLDISKFLASH# where # is an incrementing number.

Other OS – HPUX, AIX, Solaris

Each OS has its own way of representing disks. In HPUX, AIX, and SOLARIS, there is usually a block device and character device pair that can be used.

On Solaris, for instance, two directories exist in the /dev tree:

- /dev/dsk
- /dev/rdsk

The /dev/dsk location is known as a block device: a single slice or partition of a disk. /dev/rdsk, on the other hand, is a character device, which is the logical representation of the slice. When creating ASM disks, these character devices will be referenced. The location of character devices depends upon the OS:

- Solaris - */dev/rdsk*
- HPUX - */dev/rdsk*
- HPUX(True 64) - */dev/rdisk*
- AIX - */dev/rhdisk*

 Multipathing can change the location of character devices depending upon the system used. Consult the specific documentation to find the path to use for character devices.

Symbolic Links

Symbolic links can be used to ease management. For example:

```
ln -s /dev/sdb1 /dev/ocr
ln -s /dev/sdb2 /dev/voting
```

This allows logical names to be referenced during setup and makes changing paths/devices easier.

Creating ASM Diskgroups

Using OUI or DBCA, ASM instances can be graphically created over the RAC cluster. It is also possible to create the instances manually by creating ASM initialization parameter files and adding the instances to the cluster.

Once ASM has been configured, adding diskgroups can be done in DBCA, in Enterprise Manager, or at the SQL prompt. Using DBCA is extremely simple; the DBA must enter a name, a redundancy option, and choose the disks that will be part of the ASM diskgroup.

Creating ASM diskgroups at the SQL prompt is much the same, but the selections must be made through commands. For example:

```
CREATE DISKGROUP DATA
   EXTERNAL REDUNDANCY
```

```
DISK 'ORCL:DATA1', 'ORDL:DATA2';
```

This command will create a diskgroup called DATA that contains the disks marked DATA1 and DATA2 by ASMlib.

It is also possible to specify a search string for the location of the disks:

```
CREATE DISKGROUP DATA
   EXTERNAL REDUNDANCY
   DISK '/dev/rdsk/*';
```

Redundancy

In the above examples, the EXTERNAL REDUNDANCY clause was used. This means that ASM will provide no extra redundancy support and, therefore, cannot help in the case of disk failure. This is usually an option only when using RAID 1 (mirroring). However, redundancy can be set up within ASM using failure groups.

Failure groups allow a DBA to specify two pools of disks that can hold copies of each other's data. ASM allows NORMAL redundancy, in which a diskgroup is composed of two failgroups, or HIGH redundancy, in which a diskgroup is composed of three failgroups.

When files are written to the ASM diskgroup under NORMAL redundancy, the files will be written to both failgroups in a round-robin fashion. Files are read from the primary failgroup. For example:

```
CREATE DISKGROUP DATA
   NORMAL REDUNDANCY
   FAILGROUP failgrp1 DISK
     '/dev/sdb1', '/dev/sdb2'
   FAILGROUP failgrp2 DISK
     '/dev/sdc1', '/dev/sdc2';
```

In this example, a file will first go to failgrp1 and be copied to failgrp2. The next file will be written to failgrp2 and copied to failgrp1.

In Oracle 11g, the DBA can also specify Fast Failure Repair options. This means that if a disk in a failgroup is damaged, Oracle can repair the

---

damaged portion of the disk instead of cloning all files to the disk from scratch. A repair time must be set as an attribute of an ASM diskgroup, specifying how long Oracle should keep the information necessary to rebuild a damaged disk. For example:

```
ALTER DISKGROUP DATA SET ATTRIBUTE 'disk_repair_time' = '3H';
```

This command will change the maximum repair time of the DATA diskgroup to three hours, as opposed to the default of 3.6.

Another new feature of 11g AS< is preferred read groups. An ASM parameter called *asm_preferred_read_failure_groups* can be set per instance. This means that one instance in a two-node cluster can read primarily from one set of mirrored disks, and the other instance can read from another set of mirrored disks.

There are other new features of ASM in Oracle 11g that are outside the scope of this book. For more information about these features, please consult Oracle 11g New Features by Rampant Tech Press.

RAC Using NFS with Direct NFS (DNFS)

Oracle 11g comes with enhanced support for Oracle over NFS using the new Direct NFS feature. Direct NFS allows for costs savings by sticking with one connection model: the network. This allows for multipathing and unified storage. In addition, Direct NFS even works in Windows, even though Windows has no NFS support. Another nice feature of NFS is that files are directly accessible via standard OS commands like ls, mv, cp, and such.

Lastly, Oracle's Direct NFS feature allows for Direct I/O and Asynchronous I/O by default. To use Direct NFS, the client must be installed on RAC nodes. This can even be performed on nodes where Oracle RAC is already running.

The Oracle 11g Direct NFS Client is shipped with Oracle 11g. Once installed, it is very simple to put it in place:

1. Stop any RAC databases

2. Navigate to *$ORACLE_HOME/lib*

3. Move the *libodm11.so* file to a backup

4. Create a symbolic link called *libodm11.so* which uses *libnfsodm11.so* as its source

   ```
   ln -s libfsodm11.so libodm11.so
   ```

5. Start the RAC databases

Direct NFS information can then be queried from the following fixed views:

- *v$dnfs_channels*

- *v$dnfs_files*

- *v$dnfs_servers*

- *v$dnfs_stats*

> 🔔 Oracle 11g Direct NFS only works with NFS V3 compatible NAS devices.

NFS must be set up at the OS level before using the Direct NFS client. Each OS has different requirements for configuring and using NFS.

Conclusion

There are many options for data storage in a RAC environment. This is much different from the days where the only options were raw volumes or third party cluster file systems. With these options, it is possible for the DBA and System Administrators to work together to find an optimal environment for their RAC cluster.

RAC Design Considerations

Introduction

This chapter focuses on the issues that must be considered when designing for Real Application Cluster (RAC). The reasons for utilizing RAC must be well understood before a proper implementation can be achieved. These are the key reasons to use RAC:

- Spread the CPU load across multiple servers

- Provide high availability (HA)

- Take advantage of larger SGA sizes than can be accommodated by a single instance commodity server

- Scalability

Conversely, there are cases where RAC may not be an appropriate design option. It would be wise for both technical and non-technical team members to keep the following in mind when considering RAC.

- If RAC is being used as a cost savings solution, be sure to analyze both hardware and software costs

- Do not expect RAC to scale if the application will not scale on SMP

- Be realistic about the latency difference between local only memory-cache instance communication and inter-node network based multi-instance cache fusion communication

A high availability RAC design must have no single point of failure, a transparent application failover, and reliability. Failure of the local data center must also be considered. A high availability design requires attention to equipment, software, and the network.

The following sections provide a look into two key design considerations. The first is the design of the equipment needed to support a HA RAC configuration. Next, the methods of configuring RAC instances in a RAC cluster to meet performance and HA requirements will be addressed.

Designing Equipment for Real Application Clusters

The most important design feature of the equipment used in HA RAC clusters is an architecture that eliminates any single point of failure (SPF). The diagram in Figure 4.1 implements a number of design flaws that does not adhere to the definition of high availability.

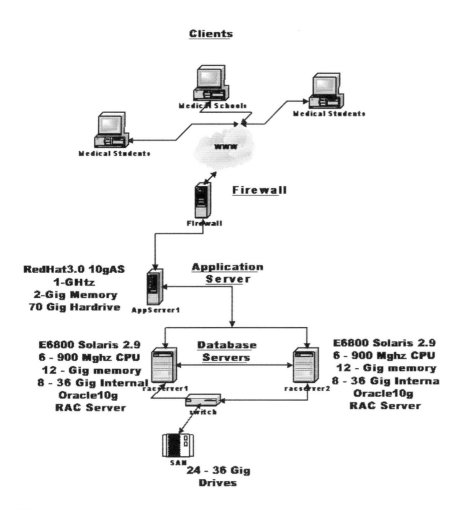

Figure 4.1: *Non-Redundant Configuration*

Figure 4.1 shows a RAC configuration. However, this configuration, other than the RAC cluster itself, has no redundancy and many single points of failure. The single points of failure are:

- Firewall
- Application Server
- Fabric Switch
- SAN array

A failure of any one of these single points will result in unscheduled downtime, no matter how well the RAC cluster is designed and tuned.

It is critical to ensure that there is no single point of failure in a high availability configuration. Figure 4.2 illustrates exactly what eliminating single points of failure means.

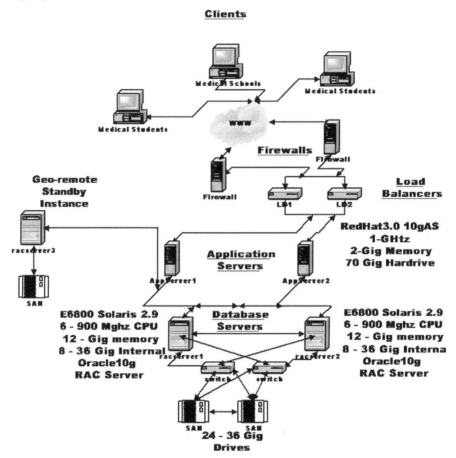

Figure 4.2: *Example of a Redundant RAC Configuration*

The system shown in Figure 4.2 has had the following redundancies added:

- Second firewall with an independent connection to the web
- Second application server

- Second fabric switch with redundant pathways

- Second SAN array

- Set of load balancers

- Geo-remote RAC Guard configuration

Now the single points of failure in Figure 4.1 have been eliminated. A third server has also been added as well as a SAN array in a geographically remote location. This third server and SAN ensure that not even a disaster at the primary location will bring the application down. The application server and firewall for this third server are not shown and may not be required if the firewalls and application servers are in a different location from the database servers.

In addition, the SAN, perhaps a Hitachi, EMC Clariion or EMC Symmetrix, should be configured using redundant disk configurations such as RAID-1 or RAID-5. It should be stressed that application performance can suffer horribly from a disk failure during either a disk rebuild with installed spares or a rebuild of the information using parity information from the other disks in a RAID-5 set.

What Are the Effects of Component Failure?

Failure of the Internet or Intranet

Internet or Intranet uptime is typically the responsibility of the Network Administrator and is not a component that a DBA usually has control over. Failure of the Internet connection, usually due to the provider, means no one outside the company Intranet can access the application. Failure of the Intranet or internal networks means no one inside the company can access the application. These components, usually comprised of multiple components, should also have built-in redundancy. As important as implementing the redundancy is, the redundancy should also be regularly tested to prove that the design functions as intended.

Failure of the Firewall

The firewall regulates the flow of traffic between networks of dissimilar trust levels. The Internet is a no trust zone, the demilitarized zone (DMZ) is an intermediate trust zone and the internal network is a trusted zone. A proper firewall configuration will implement a default-deny rule-set and only allow network connections that have been explicitly set. No firewall is needed if the database is strictly on an internal network with no connection to the Internet. However, if users access the database through or from a non-trusted zone, such as the Internet, and there is only one firewall, a failure will prevent anyone outside the firewall from contacting the database. Internal users, those inside the firewall on the same network, may still have access.

Failure of the Application Server

The application server usually serves the web pages, reports, forms, or other interfaces to the users of the system. If there is only a single application server and it goes down, even if the database is fully functional, there is no application to run against it. A failed application server without redundancy means no one can use the database, even if all other components are still functional.

Failure of the Database Server

The failure of the database server is the one failure that is taken care of in a normal RAC configuration. Failure of a single database server leads to failover of the connections to the surviving node. While not a critical failure that will result in loss of the system, a single server failure means a reduction in performance and capacity. Of course, a catastrophic failure of both servers will result in total loss of service.

If the application is mission critical, consider sizing the servers so that a surviving node can handle the load of the failed instance without a noticeable reduction of service.

The servers will have disk controllers or interfaces that connect through the switches to the SAN arrays. These controllers or interfaces should also be made redundant and have multiple channels per controller or interface. In addition, multiple network interface cards (NICs) should also be redundant with at least a single spare to take the place of either the network connection card or the cluster interconnect should a failure occur.

Failure of the Fabric Switch

The fabric switch allows multiple hosts to access the SAN array. These switches communicate via FCP (fibre channel protocol). A fabric switch is different than a typical Ethernet switch because the protocol is different and FCP supports redundant paths between multiple components, creating a mesh network. This design is important for I/O failover and I/O scalability. Failure of one redundant fabric switch can result in loss of performance. Complete fabric switch failure will result in a full RAC crash. If the RAC shared disk is unavailable, the Oracle RAC instances are worthless.

SAN Failure

Failure of a single drive can result in severe performance degradation. During a disk failure in a RAID-5 array, the replacement or hot spare disk has to be rebuilt using parity information found on the surviving drives in the RAID-5 set. During this RAID-5 rebuild process the RAID-5 I/O performance will suffer by as much as 400-1000 percent.

Failure of a RAID-0+1 drive has little effect on performance as its mirror drive takes over while the hot spare is rebuilt on an "on available" basis. In a RAID-5 array, the drives are usually set up in an n+1 configuration, meaning n drives in a stripe set and one parity drive.

When a drive fails, there must be an immediate spare available to replace it; even if the hot spare is not available, a cold spare should be available. If the hot spare has already activated and a second drive is lost, the entire array is in jeopardy. Most of these arrays use hot pluggable drives meaning they can, in time of failure, be replaced with the system running.

NICs and HBAs

A HA RAC design will have many physical network connections in order to provided true redundancy. Note that all of the physical connections are not shown in diagram 4.2. In an implementation, each component is physically connected usually via a network interface card (NIC) or host bus adapter (HBA) interface.

NIC or HBA interfaces should be the fastest possible, especially in the case of the cluster interconnect and disk connect. For example, using Gigabit Ethernet for the interconnect seems very fast when compared to older network technologies. However, a single Gigabit Ethernet NIC should not be considered more than adequate in all cases. The Oracle RAC design may require NIC teaming/bonding. Upgrading to 10 Gigabit Ethernet is another option to increase bandwidth. 10 Gigabit Ethernet speed is 1,250 MB/s versus Gigabit Ethernet's 125 MB/s.

Failed NIC interfaces result in the loss of that component unless a second NIC card is failed over to immediately. A failure of a non-redundant HBA results in loss of connection to the disk array. Redundancy is the key. Not having multiple NICs and HBAs on a mission critical Oracle RAC is a poor design.

Failure of the InterConnect Switch / Memory

The interconnect switch is a core part of the RAC Architecture. The switch should be an enterprise grade managed switch. 10 Gigabit Ethernet switches are not cheap, but could increase performance significantly.

Various server vendors provide advanced memory fault protection features such as Error Correcting Code (ECC), online spares, and mirroring.

Provide Redundancy at Each Level

It is easy to see that redundancy at the hardware level is vital. At each level of the hardware layout an alternate access path must be available. Duplicating all equipment and configuring the automatic failover capabilities of the hardware reduce the chances of hardware failure to virtually nil.

By providing the required levels of redundancy, the system becomes highly available. Once there is an HA configuration, it is up to the manager to plan any software or application upgrades to further reduce application downtime. In Oracle Database 11g, rolling upgrades are supported, further increasing reliability. It is highly recommended that all upgrades be tested on non-production systems first. Oracle 11g provides a new testing tool called Database Replay. More information about the Enterprise Edition Database Replay capabilities can be found at oracle.com.

At the SAN level, appropriate duplication software should be used to ensure the SAN arrays are kept synchronous. Oracle Database 11g allows for use of Oracle Automatic Storage Management or ASM. ASM can provide striping to improve availability.

DBA and User Error Protection

Oracle provides many data protection utilities and features that should be tested and understood so that an emergency does not involve a learning curve. RMAN, of course, is Oracle's backup utility. Flashback is new as of Oracle 10g. Here is a list of the various components of the Flashback package:

- Flashback Query
- Flashback Version Query
- Flashback Transaction Query
- DBMS_FLASHBACK package

- Flashback Transaction

- Flashback Data Archive (Oracle Total Recall)

- Flashback Table

- Flashback Drop (Recycle Bin)

- Flashback Database

Designing for High Performance

The next section is an in-depth look at several of the details a database architect may need to consider when designing for high performance. Some of the details are more relevant when the number of users is greater than one thousand. However, it is good for any database architect to understand the scores of variables that may affect performance on larger-sized deployments.

As an example to visualize how each software and hardware component needs to be able to continue to function as the number of transactions per minute (TPM) increases, the major components of one of the fastest airplanes in the world, the SR-71 will be briefly analyzed.

The major structural parts of an SR-71 (or any fixed-wing plane) consist of:

- Wing ribs (forms the skeletal shape of the wing)

- Spars (main structural part of the wing, defines length of the wing)

- Frame (forms the skeletal shape of the plane body)

- Longerons (main structural part of the fuselage, front to rear)

- Skin

As an SR-71's speed doubles from 100 mph to 200 mph and finally reaches its top speed of Mach 3.2, the strength of the wing ribs, spars, frame, longerons, and skin all need to scale to handle the structural demands that the powerful Pratt Whitney engines require. In a similar way, as a database's TPM (transactions per minute) doubles, the CPUs, memory, disks, application and such all need to scale in unison. If one component becomes the bottleneck, the huge capacity of the other components is irrelevant until the bottleneck is removed. Hopefully, the bottleneck will be addressed before it crashes!

Becoming a subject-matter expert of database performance design takes time and real world experience. It is also an iterative process. There is no magic in any database vendor's source code. The cost-based optimizers in today's modern RDBMSs (Relational Database Management Systems) all depend on statistics to make decisions. Many times, however, the best solution to a performance problem is found outside of the database and in the Application design. Application design plays a major role in determining user response times. All the unscalable application design mistakes that have been seen over the years cannot be listed here, but here are a few things to keep in mind.

Unscalable Design Mistakes

These unscalable design mistakes should be avoided.

- Unused indexes
- Over-normalization
- Unnecessary 15-way table joins
- Unnecessary frequent database connects and disconnects
- Unnecessary queries against gigantic tables
- Poor server I/O optimization
- Bad disk I/O configuration
- Insufficient RAM
- SGA too small
- SGA way too big
- Not using bind variables
- Developers coding the same SQL using different capitalization

- Not understanding performance related init parameters
- Coding features into the application that the database can do better and faster
- Complex views to reference other complex views
- Lack of change management procedures
- Repeatedly reading static data when data could be cached
- Memory leaks
- Committing too often / Poor transaction management
- DBA's failure to monitor their database
- Failing to distribute load across multiple RAC instances
- Failing to segregate load types (DS vs. OLTP)
- Failing to monitor for heavy interconnect traffic

Hardware Planning

Knowing the hardware details of similar large and scalable installations, e.g. from past experience, is one of the best ways to ensure the new architecture will also scale. Designing without a similar system to use as a point of reference could mean that one is designing in the dark. It would be wise to open up a dialog with a capacity-planning expert that works for one's hardware vendor. Dell, HP, IBM, SUN and others all have capacity planning experts. Besides, Oracle recommends that all RAC implementers notify their hardware vendors that the purchase is intended for a RAC system. Be sure to listen to the technical expertise of the vendor engineers, not the salesman.

Of course, online resources can be very helpful. One of the best Oracle white papers involving RAC and I/O is Building a Multi-Terabyte Data Warehouse Using Linux and RAC. This white paper is a must read.

Once the hardware is up and running, be sure to take advantage of the new Oracle 11g CALIBRATE_IO procedure. This procedure will help determine if the I/O levels are as high as is expected.

Below is a list of hardware components that may need to be considered when designing for performance. The bullet points are not a comprehensive list, but are a starting point for making hardware purchase decisions.

CPUs

- Architecture
- Speed
- L1, L2, L3 cache
- Number of cores
- Supported operating systems

Memory

- Size
- Speed
- Type
- Mirroring
- RAID
- ECC
- Number of slots on motherboard
- Motherboard maximum
- Note swap file size is determined by memory size

System Bus

- Speed

PCI

- PCI-X
- PCI-Express
- PCI-E x4
- PCI-E x8
- PCI-E X16

Disks

- Size
- Speed
- Type
- Consider sum of I/O of all instances
- Can the disk architecture easily scale
- Disk testing tools
  - dd
  - ORION
  - IOZone

Raid Configuration

- Oracle recommends not using RAID-5 for redo logs
- Separate archive logs from redo logs
- See Metalink NOTE: 45635.1

Network Adapters

- Speed
- Latency

- NIC bonding

Host Bus Adapters

- Speed
- Path Redundancy

Fibre Switches

- Speed
- Zoning
- Number of ports

Storage Area Network

- Cache size
  - SAN cache is good, but salespeople typically exaggerate the benefits
  - SAN cache cannot mask all disk I/O problems
- Number of disks
- Speed
- Many different business continuity features

SCSI Controllers

- Cache size

Software Planning

If the application software is provided by a vendor, verify that the implementation is not the first RAC implementation. Ask the vendor if RAC is a recommended solution for the application software that is intended to be used.

Database Planning

Below is a list of database details that may need to be considered when designing for performance. This is not a comprehensive list, but can be used as a starting point when making high performance database design plans.

Indexes

- Full table scans on big tables can be extremely expensive
- Index design can be iterative
- Covered indexes
- Index types
  - B-tree
  - Bitmap
  - Function-based
  - Partitioned
  - Reverse key
- Document plan for rebuilding indexes as needed
- Remove unused indexes
  - Unused indexes are one of the top reasons for poor Oracle performance (according to Burleson Consulting)
- New 11g invisible index feature
- Monitoring usage feature

Enable index usage monitoring on one of the indexes

```
alter index table_idx monitoring usage;
```

Query v$object_usage:

```
select
    index_name,
```

```
        table_name,
        used
from
        v$object_usage;
```

Disable index usage monitoring:

```
alter index table_idx nomonitoring usage;
```

Tables

- Materialized views

- Clustered tables

Temporary Tablespaces

- Used for sorting

- Oracle recommends using locally managed temp tablespaces with UNIFORM extent size 1MB

- Document plan for monitoring *v$sort_usage*

Redo Log Files

- Do not use RAID-5

- Separate from archive logs

- Put redo log files on separate disks from other files, especially archive log files

- Too few redo log groups makes it hard for the archive log process to keep up

- Oracle advises redo log file size ranging from 100 MB to a few gigabytes

- A good indicator is to size the redo log files to switch logs no more than once every twenty minutes

- Multiple log file copies on separate disks is an Oracle best practice

- Document plan for monitoring redo log files

Designing for High Performance   **133**

Archive Log Files

- Archive log mode is required to preserve all transactions
- Separate from redo log files
- Too few redo log groups makes it hard for the archive log process to keep up
- Default is two archive processes
- Oracle starts additional ARCn processes as needed
- LOG_ARCHIVE_DEST_n can be used to multiplex log files up to 10 local or remote destinations
- Document plan for monitoring archive log files

Control Files

- At least two files on different disks

Oracle Managed Files

- Simplifies file administration
- Only need to specify the directory path
- Specify one location for data files
- Specify up to five locations for control files and redo log files
- Not available for raw disks

Data Block Size

- If one is unsure what size to use, use 8 KB

Log Files

- 11g has new log file destination
- Determined by DIAGNOSTIC_DEST parameter

Better Performance on RAC

Here are some tips to obtain better performance on a RAC system.

- Assign transactions with similar data access characteristics to specific nodes

- Adjust table rows-per-block (RPB) when necessary

- Automate free space allocation and deallocation through the use of locally managed tablespaces

- Using sequences properly for RAC

  - Cache

  - Non-ordered

- Optimize SQL

- Understanding the workload on the system and planning the application to properly utilize resources

Compartmenting Transactions to Specific Nodes

One method of reducing traffic between instances is to isolate the transactions that use a specific data set to a specific server in the RAC cluster. In a multi-use instance that contains multiple applications, one can isolate each application's user logins to a specific node. For example, sales users use the sales node, accounting users use the accounting node, and so on. In the case of a node failure, the users switch to one of the other nodes.

This compartmenting of transactions is difficult to implement for a large, multi-use RAC database where many different groups of users use each of the applications on the RAC cluster. In the case of a multi-use instance that is used by almost all corporate users, other techniques must be employed to optimize performance. High-end disk hardware such as RamSan, cacheFX and most recently, Oracle's Exadata, deliver impressive I/O rates.

Proper Sequence Usage

If not used properly, sequences can be a major headache in RAC. Non-cached sequences can be the cause of major performance issues on RAC. Another major performance issue can occur if the cached sequence's *cache_value* is set too low. Tom Kyte wrote on his website, asktom.oracle.com, the following about proper sequence usage.

> "You would be amazed what setting a sequence cache via alter sequence to 100,000 or more can do during a large load -- amazed."

Note, however, that cache values are lost during shutdown. Generally speaking, sequences should be either CACHED or ORDERED, but not both. The preferred sequence is a CACHED, non-ordered sequence. If the ordering of sequences is forced, performance in a RAC environment will suffer unless ordering the sequence to a single node in the RAC cluster isolates insert activity.

Oracle 11g RAC Sequence Example

Create the sequence.

```
SQL> create sequence seq_rac_test cache 50;

Sequence created.
```

Select the sequence from node 1.

```
SQL> select seq_rac_test.nextval from dual;

NEXTVAL
----------
1
```

Again.

```
SQL> /

NEXTVAL
----------
```

```
2
```

Again.

```
SQL> /

NEXTVAL
----------
3
```

Again.

```
SQL> /

NEXTVAL
----------
4
```

Now select the sequence from node 2.

```
SQL> select seq_rac_test.nextval from dual;

NEXTVAL
----------
51
```

Again.

```
SQL> /

NEXTVAL
----------
52
```

Again.

```
SQL> /

NEXTVAL
----------
53
```

Again.

```
SQL> /

NEXTVAL
----------
54
```

Select again from node 1 when NEXTVAL is near the cache maximum of 50.

```
SQL> /

NEXTVAL
----------
48
```

Again.

```
SQL> /

NEXTVAL
----------
49
```

Again.

```
SQL> /

NEXTVAL
----------
50
```

Again.

```
SQL> /

NEXTVAL
----------
101
```

As can be seen, since node 2 has already cached values 51-100, it is logical that node 1 will then cache 101-150. Using the order clause when creating the sequence will guarantee sequence order across all RAC instances, but will likely cause performance problems.

Another method to optimize the use of sequences is to use a staggered sequence insert trigger. A staggered sequence insert trigger is a specific constant added to the sequence value based on the instance number. This isolates each set of inserts and prevents inadvertent attempts to use the same sequence number. An example of a staggered sequence insert trigger is shown in the following script:

```
CREATE TRIGGER insert_EMP_PK
 BEFORE insert ON EMP
 FOR EACH ROW
DECLARE
 INST_ID NUMBER;
 SEQ_NUM NUMBER;
 INST_SEQ_ID NUMBER;
BEGIN
 select
    INSTANCE_NUMBER INTO INST_ID
  FROM
    V$INSTANCE;
  select
    EMP_ID_SEQ.NEXTVAL INTO SEQ_NUM
  FROM
    DUAL;
  INST_SEQ_ID:=(INST_ID-1)*100000 + SEQ_NUM;
  :NEW.EMP_ID:=INST_SEQ_ID;
END;.
```

A staggered sequence trigger will insert the values into indexes such that each instance's values are staggered to prevent index node intra-node transfers. The formula to allow this is:

```
index key = (instance_number -1)* 100000+ Sequence number
```

One of the best ways to determine if sequences are a bottleneck on the system is to simply run the following query.

```
SELECT LAST_NUMBER FROM DBA_SEQUENCES WHERE SEQUENCE_NAME = 'X'
```

The above query will show the last sequence number that has been written to disk. A safe rule to follow is to ensure the LAST_NUMBER value changes only a few times per day. If the LAST_NUMBER is changing constantly, make sure the sequence is cached. If the sequence is cached, keep increasing the cache value until the LAST_NUMBER stabilizes.

In some applications, the sequence numbers used must be sequential. An example would be the line numbers for a purchase order or perhaps check numbers for an automatic check printer. In this case, a sequence table may have to be used to store the highest sequence number. The value is read from the sequence table, increased by one, and then updated. While all of this occurs, the row for the sequence being used is locked, thus no one else can use it. If this type of logic must be used, the table should be placed in a tablespace with a small 2048 block size.

Conclusion

Great care must be taken to select the fastest interface and network components to get optimal performance from the cluster interconnect.

Designing for true high availability starts with redundant hardware. If there are multiple single-points of failure, the finest RAC implementation in the known universe will do little to achieve high availability.

The response time and throughput requirements placed on the system by service-level agreements and customer/client expectations ultimately determine whether a data and functional partitioning strategy should be implemented and how stringent the strategy must be. The response time and throughput needs for the application also determine how much effort needs to be invested to achieve an optimal database design.

To determine how to allocate work to particular instances, start with a careful analysis of the system's workload. This analysis must consider:

- System resource consumption by functional area
- Data access distributions by functional area
- Functional dependencies between application software components

Proper implementation of a strategy that considers these points will make the system more robust and scalable.

The old 80/20 rule applies here; 80% or more of the overhead results from 20% or less of the workload. If the 20% is fixed by observing some simple guidelines, tangible benefits can be achieved with minimal effort. Workload problems can be corrected by implementing any or all of the following:

- Use Oracle automated free list management or define free list groups for partitioned, as well as non-partitioned, data that is frequently modified

- Use read-only tablespaces wherever data remains constant

- Use Oracle sequences to generate unique numbers and set the CACHE parameter to a high value, if needed

- Use sequence staggering to help prevent index block contention

- If possible, reduce concurrent changes to index blocks. However, if index key values are not modified by multiple instances, or if the modification rate is not excessive, the overhead may be acceptable. In extreme cases, techniques like physical table partitioning can be applied.

References

Maximum Availability Architecture
Oracle's Recipe For Building An Unbreakable System,
Ashish Prabhu, Douglas Utzig

High Availability Systems Group, Server Technologies, Oracle Corporation

Real-World Performance of Oracle9i Release 2, Andrew Holdsworth Director of Real World Performance, Server Technologies, Oracle Corporation.

Building Highly Available Database Servers Using Oracle Real Application Clusters: RAC Performance Experts Reveal All.
Barb Lundhild, Michael Zoll

Sequences-in-oracle-10g-rac,
Mark Backhouse

Metalink.com
Oracle.com

Oracle Grid & Real Application Clusters

RAC Administration Toolbox

Administration of a RAC Environment

There are many tools built into Oracle to help a DBA administer an Oracle database. The two most popular tools are:

- SQL*Plus

- Oracle Enterprise Manager

These tools provide nearly everything a DBA needs to create, configure, and manage the database. Through SQL*Plus, using Oracle's built-in DBMS packages, RDBMS scripts, and DDL commands, nearly every aspect of traditional database and instance management can be performed.

In addition, there are several other tools useful for the single instance DBA:

- Oracle Universal Installer (OUI)

- Database Configuration Assistant (DBCA)

- Network Configuration Assistant (NETCA)

- Listener Control (LSNRCTL)

- Automatic Diagnostic Repository Command Interpreter (ADRCI)

- Datafile Verification (DBVERIFY)

- DB ID Changer (DBNEWID)

- Datapump Export/Import (expdp/impdp)

- Original Export/Import (exp/imp)

- Enterprise Manager Configuration Assistant (EMCA)

- SQL Loader (SQLLDR)

Most DBAs will have some experience using these programs to manage a single instance database.

RAC also uses these tools as they are part of the core toolset provided by Oracle. For instance, Datapump is a logical export that is useful no matter how many instances make up the Oracle system; exported data is universal across all nodes. However, because of the extra components of a RAC system, there are several other tools that are built into clusterware and Oracle that allow more specific administration of a RAC environment. These will be covered later in the chapter.

What is the Difference?

RAC contains many different components and concepts that are not part of the standard database setup, including:

- Clusterware
- Public IP, VIP, and Interconnect
- OCR (Oracle Cluster Registry)
- Voting Disk
- Nodeapps (GSD, ONS, VIP)
- Database
- Clustered listener and advanced failover
- ASM storage
- Service administration (ASM, instances, services)

Oracle's core functionality has been changed to allow for RAC enabled systems.

Oracle Universal Installer

The Oracle Universal Installer (OUI) is one of the core components built into Oracle. The Java implementation of the OUI has been around for a long time and is used to install any Oracle product, including clusterware and the Oracle RDBMS engine itself.

In Oracle 11g RAC, clusterware is installed through OUI. OUI has the ability to install and configure all components of the clusterware software, in addition to copying of local components across the cluster to other nodes.

This means that when clusterware is installed, OUI will be able to take the local implementation of the software and copy it to all nodes designated as cluster members. Because of this, clusterware must only be installed once; the installation will propagate to all other nodes.

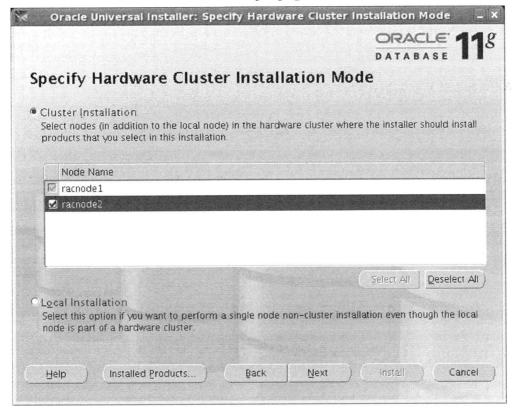

Figure 5.1: *Clusterware Node Selection*

OUI 11g is also able to assist in the configuration of ASM and RAC databases during install time by calling RAC enabled tools after installation. For instance, it is common to use OUI to create a listener and install and configure ASM in order to have a smoother database creation afterwards.

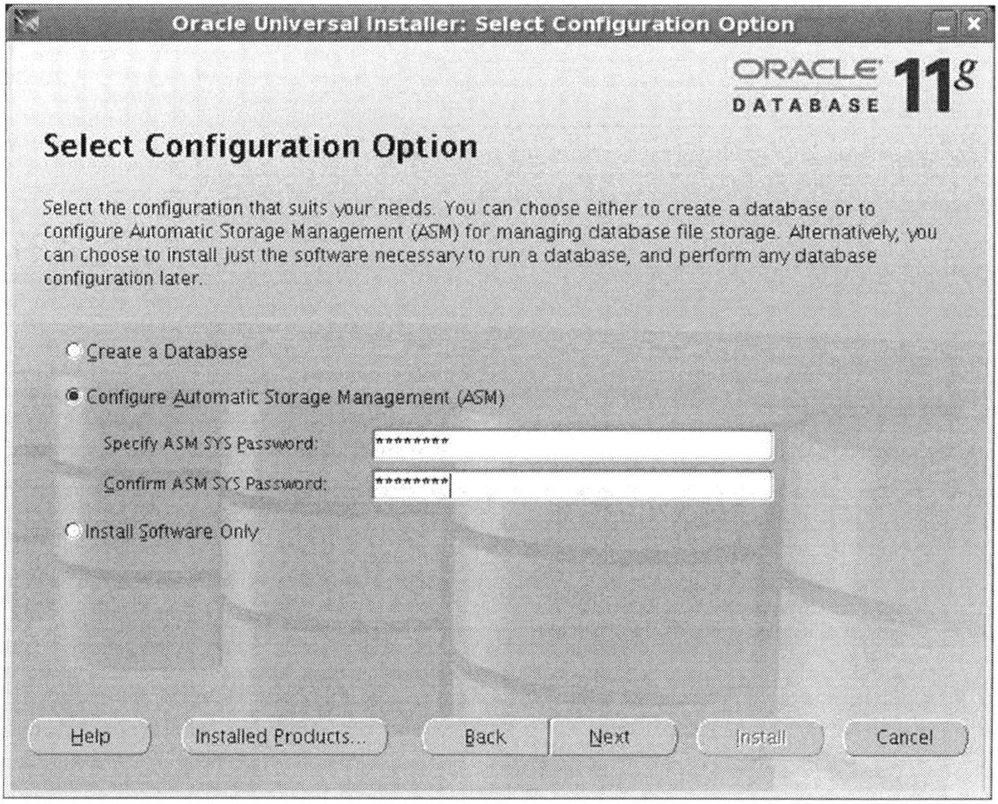

Figure 5.2: *ASM Setup in OUI*

DBCA

Like OUI, the Database Configuration Assistant is able to work across multiple nodes. Using DBCA, it is possible to create or delete a RAC database, add instances to a RAC cluster, and administer ASM over all nodes of a RAC cluster.

> 🔔 Oracle 11g DBCA does not have the ability to perform Services management as did Oracle 10g DBCA.

When Oracle Clusterware is installed and RAC services are configured and started, DBCA will become cluster-aware. This means that any databases created can optionally be created across multiple nodes of the RAC cluster.

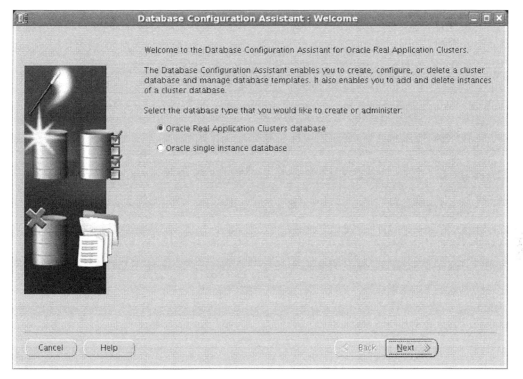

Figure 5.3: *DBCA is RAC Aware*

Additionally, when creating a database using DBCA in RAC, the database name screen is slightly different. A global database name can be entered along with a SID prefix; meaning that the instances in the clustered database will have a number after the SID prefix.

For instance, if the RAC database RACDB is named on a two-node cluster, the instances of the database would be named RACDB1 and RACDB2.

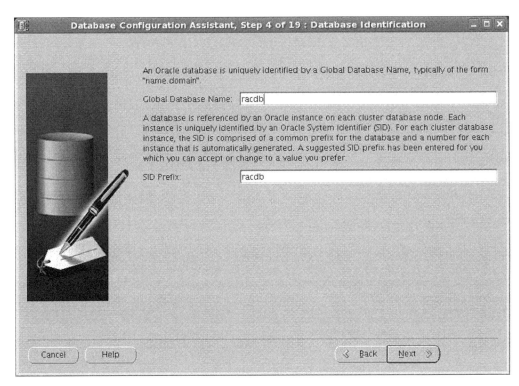

An Oracle database is uniquely identified by a Global Database Name, typically of the form "name.domain".

Global Database Name: racdb

A database is referenced by an Oracle instance on each cluster database node. Each instance is uniquely identified by an Oracle System Identifier (SID). For each cluster database instance, the SID is comprised of a common prefix for the database and a number for each instance that is automatically generated. A suggested SID prefix has been entered for you which you can accept or change to a value you prefer.

SID Prefix: racdb

Cancel   Help   Back   Next

Figure 5.4: *DBCA Database Name Entry*

Once the database configuration is complete, Oracle will create the database and all instances across the nodes of the cluster.

SQL*Plus

SQL*Plus also has useful capabilities that ease RAC management. These include both *v$* views and built in tools.

v$ and gv$ Views

Any Oracle instance has *v$* views, which read from *x$* views, which can read from a combination of base tables, RAM areas, processes, or the control file. *gv$* views are just the same, except they span across all nodes of the cluster. Each *gv$* view has an INST_ID column that notes the instance on which the record belongs.

v$instance is a very commonly used view that shows quick details about the Oracle instance. *gv$instance* shows status on all nodes of the cluster and is a great way to know which nodes are up or down!

v$sql_plan and *v$sqlarea* can be used to find queries on a variety of criteria: join methods, index usage, buffer gets or disk reads and more. Using *gv$sql_plan* and *gv$sqlarea*, it is possible to find out which nodes certain SQL has affected.

Another useful view is *gv$session*. This view gives information about all connected sessions across every Oracle node. When coupled with *gv$session_wait*, it is possible to find specific details about the wait interface by session. With *gv$session*, *gv$session_wait*, and *gv$sqlarea* it is possible to really delve deep into object usage and bottlenecks.

> 🔔 If the database was created manually with the CREATE DATABASE command, one will have to create the cluster views using the CATCLUST.SQL script. Run this script as SYSDBA. It is located in $ORACLE_HOME/rdbms/admin.

In addition to the *gv$* views, Oracle 11g offers three built-in statistics and analysis tools that are RAC aware: AWR, ADDM, and ASH.

Automatic Workload Repository (AWR)

Using Enterprise Manager or the *awrrpt.sql* script, a DBA can generate an AWR report that contains specific RAC information. AWR is automatically configured to take snapshots of each instance in the cluster. Using this snapshot information, a report can be generated that gives instance-specific information along with cluster-wide information.

For instance, using AWR in a RAC environment, it is possible to easily find the ratio of local vs. cache fusion block gets for a given snapshot period. This kind of data can help a DBA diagnose performance or stability issues.

Automatic Database Diagnostic Monitor (ADDM)

ADDM was introduced in Oracle 10g. It takes the AWR statistics a step further by analyzing the data and creating a report of findings; plain English solutions to system issues.

In Oracle 11g, ADDM has been extended to include RAC. As such, it provides information on the entire cluster including latency on the cluster interconnect, global cache hot blocks, and other RAC specific topics that span multiple nodes. ADDM can still create single instance reports or database wide reports which can span all instances accessing a single RAC database.

Active Session History (ASH)

Active Session History (ASH) contains data specific to active sessions connected to the Oracle instances of a cluster. Every session that performs work will have statistics, wait events, and work details saved into the ASH framework. From this framework ASH reports can be generated, showing session performance for a given time period. These reports are highly beneficial with tuning wait events that happen during a specific time.

In Oracle 11g RAC, ASH reports contain specific RAC information in the form of Top Cluster Events and Top Remote Instance sections.

The Top Cluster Events section of an ASH report will contain all events during the given timeframe that are specific to Oracle RAC.

> Tip: If cluster wait events contribute heavily to overall system wait, this section is useful to drill down into the specific cluster waits causing the overall issue.

Sometimes it is good to know which instance in a cluster is waiting the longest during a specific period. The Top Remote Instance section breaks down cluster wait events by instance number which makes it easy to understand which nodes performed specific amounts of work.

SQL*Plus Conclusion

There are many tools that can be used right from the SQL* prompt in a RAC environment. It is worth noting that most of these tools can also be accessed through Enterprise Manager for those that do not like to work at the command prompt. AWR, ADDM, and ASH specifically are highly supported through Enterprise Manager in the Performance tab and Advisor Central.

RAC Specific Tools

Oracle Clusterware 11g includes extra tools that are strictly for the purpose of managing a RAC cluster. For the most part, these tools are low level; they interface directly with the clusterware daemons, OCR, the voting disk, or the interconnect. Because of the complex nature of RAC and the multitude of low level components involved, it is important to understand how to use these tools.

Some tools, on the other hand, are higher level. For instance, tools for service registration, starting and stopping services, and displaying services are included that will be in constant use.

Low Level Tools

Olsnodes

The olsnodes program is used to provide node membership information. It is a quick way to find which nodes are part of the cluster.

> Tip: Olsnodes is also useful to find out if there is a low level issue with the clusterware daemons. If olsnodes cannot be run, then something is definitely wrong!

Running olsnodes in its basic form with no parameters simply shows a list of nodes in the cluster:

```
[root@racnode1 bin]# olsnodes
racnode1
racnode2
```

Olsnodes is especially useful using the following options:

- -i - includes VIP information
- -n - includes node number
- -p - includes private interconnect information
- -v - verbose mode

```
[root@racnode1 bin]# olsnodes -i -n -p
racnode1    1     racnode1-priv      racnode1-vip
racnode2    2     racnode2-priv      racnode2-vip
```

OIFCFG

OIFCFG is used to configure and query the clusterware network information. It can be used to drop or add public or private interfaces, change network adapters, or list information about the network.

The four main commands of this tool are:

- iflist - returns interfaces that can be configured
- setif - sets an interface type for a given interface
- getif - displays configured interfaces
- delif - deletes configured interface information

Additionally, the following parameters will be used depending on the requirements of the command:

- -node *node_name* or -global - This parameter allows either one node to be configured, or the entire subnet
- -if *if_name* and *subnet* - Interface name and subnet on the system

- -type *if_type* - Type of the interface. Can be set to *cluster_interconnect*, public, or storage.

When the -global option is used instead of a *node_name*, configuration will take place for all nodes of the cluster on the same interface and subnet. For example, if two nodes are members of a cluster, each using *eth1* as the cluster interconnect with IP addresses on the same subnet, the -global option will allow for changes to the entire subnet.

Querying Interfaces

```
$ oifcfg getif
eth0 192.168.1.0          global          public
eth1 10.1.1.0             global          cluster_interconnect
```

The two global interfaces listed by the *getif* command show the IP subnet for the interface. Public IPs on the cluster must use *eth0* and be in the 192.168.1.0 subnet range, and private IPs must use *eth1* and be in the 10.1.1.0 subnet range.

Deleting Interfaces

To delete a given interface, the *delif* command can be used:

```
$ oifcfg delif -global eth1/10.1.1.0
```

To delete all interfaces, use the -global option without specifying an interface or subnet:

```
$ oifcfg delif -global
```

Adding Interfaces

To add an interface, the *setif* command can be used. This can add both public and private interfaces.

```
$ oifcfg setif -global eth1/10.1.1.0:cluster_interconnect
```

> Note: When the public interface is changed, nodeapps must be reconfigured. This will be discussed later in the chapter under the srvctl command.

OCRCONFIG

OCRCONFIG is used to manage the Cluster Registry file in a RAC environment. Using this tool, backups of the OCR can be viewed, taken, and restored. By default, the OCR is backed up every four hours. However, in Oracle 11g it is possible to take manual backups of the OCR in the event that maintenance needs to take place.

Taking an OCR Backup

- Set backup location with the *-backuploc* command.

  ```
  ocrconfig -backuploc /u01/app/oracle/backups/ocr
  ```

- Take a backup with the *-manualbackup* command.

  ```
  Ocrconfig -manualbackup
  ```

To view the backups that have been taken, use the *-showbackup* option.

These backups are useful in the event of an issue where the OCR becomes corrupt or unusable. The backup OCR file can be restored with the *-restore* option.

Example:

```
[root@racnode1 bin]# ./ocrconfig -backuploc /u01/app/oracle/backups/ocr
[root@racnode1 bin]# ./ocrconfig -manualbackup
racnode1      2008/09/30 21:05:17
/u01/app/oracle/backups/ocr/backup_20080930_210517.ocr
[root@racnode1 bin]# ./ocrconfig -showbackup
racnode1      2008/09/30 21:05:17
/u01/app/oracle/backups/ocr/backup_20080930_210517.ocr
```

 The *-export* option is good to export the contents of the OCR. Using ocrconfig *-export* and the *strings* command, every facet of a cluster's setup can be viewed.

Another highly useful *ocrconfig* option is the -replace option, which allows the replacement of the ocr or ocrmirror location.

Command use:

```
ocrconfig -replace ocr destination_file|disk
ocrconfig -replace ocrmirror destination_file|disk
```

Either a file on a cluster file system or a disk device can be specified for either the OCR or the OCR Mirror location.

OCRCHECK

OCRCHECK is a basic utility that displays useful information about the Cluster Registry. This information includes:

- OCR Version
- OCR Total/Used/Available Space
- ID
- OCR File Name

```
[root@racnode1 bin]# ./ocrcheck
Status of Oracle Cluster Registry is as follows :
        Version                   :           2
        Total space (kbytes)      :     1048296
        Used space (kbytes)       :        3804
        Available space (kbytes)  :     1044492
        ID                        :  1880797558
        Device/File Name          :    /dev/sdb
                            Device/File integrity check succeeded

                            Device/File not configured

        Cluster registry integrity check succeeded
```

OCRDUMP

OCRDUMP provides information about data within the OCR. Information can be written either to a file or to standard output, possibly in XML format. Optionally, a backup file can be specified with the -*backupfile* parameter, which will analyze a backup file instead of the live OCR.

Options:

- *-stdout* - Dump to screen

- *file_name* - Dump to file

  - If the *-stdout* parameter and *file_name* are omitted, the command will dump a file in the local directory called OCRDUMPFILE.

- *-xml* - Use XML output

- *-backupfile* - Specify a backupfile to analyze

Example output:

```
[root@racnode1 bin]# ./ocrdump
[root@racnode1 bin]# head -30 OCRDUMPFILE
09/30/2008 21:37:38
./ocrdump.bin

[SYSTEM]
UNDEF :
SECURITY : {USER_PERMISSION : PROCR_ALL_ACCESS, GROUP_PERMISSION :
PROCR_READ, OTHER_PERMISSION : PROCR_READ, USER_NAME : root, GROUP_NAME :
root}

[SYSTEM.css]
UNDEF :
SECURITY : {USER_PERMISSION : PROCR_ALL_ACCESS, GROUP_PERMISSION :
PROCR_READ, OTHER_PERMISSION : PROCR_READ, USER_NAME : root, GROUP_NAME :
root}

[SYSTEM.css.interfaces]
UNDEF :
SECURITY : {USER_PERMISSION : PROCR_ALL_ACCESS, GROUP_PERMISSION :
PROCR_CREATE_SUB_KEY, OTHER_PERMISSION : PROCR_READ, USER_NAME : oracle,
GROUP_NAME : oinstall}

[SYSTEM.css.interfaces.global]
UNDEF :
SECURITY : {USER_PERMISSION : PROCR_ALL_ACCESS, GROUP_PERMISSION :
PROCR_ALL_ACCESS, OTHER_PERMISSION : PROCR_READ, USER_NAME : oracle,
GROUP_NAME : oinstall}

[SYSTEM.css.interfaces.global.eth0]
UNDEF :
SECURITY : {USER_PERMISSION : PROCR_ALL_ACCESS, GROUP_PERMISSION :
PROCR_ALL_ACCESS, OTHER_PERMISSION : PROCR_READ, USER_NAME : oracle,
GROUP_NAME : oinstall}

[SYSTEM.css.interfaces.global.eth0.192|d168|d1|d0]
UNDEF :
SECURITY : {USER_PERMISSION : PROCR_ALL_ACCESS, GROUP_PERMISSION :
PROCR_ALL_ACCESS, OTHER_PERMISSION : PROCR_READ, USER_NAME : oracle,
GROUP_NAME : oinstall}
```

```
[SYSTEM.css.interfaces.global.eth0.192|d168|d1|d0.1]
ORATEXT : public
SECURITY : {USER_PERMISSION : PROCR_ALL_ACCESS, GROUP_PERMISSION :
PROCR_ALL_ACCESS, OTHER_PERMISSION : PROCR_READ, USER_NAME : oracle,
GROUP_NAME : oinstall}
```

CRSCTL

CRSCTL is an action packed program that allows many different operations related to the clusterware software. These operations include the enabling/disabling of clusterware on startup, replacing or moving voting disks, checking the viability of the cluster, and advanced debugging.

The *crsctl* command by itself prints the specifications of the program:

```
Usage: crsctl check crs - checks the viability of the Oracle Clusterware
        crsctl check cssd        - checks the viability of Cluster Synchronization
Services
        crsctl check crsd        - checks the viability of Cluster Ready Services
        crsctl check evmd        - checks the viability of Event Manager
        crsctl check cluster [-node <nodename>] - checks the viability of CSS across
nodes
        crsctl set css <parameter> <value> - sets a parameter override
        crsctl get css <parameter> - sets the value of a Cluster Synchronization
Services parameter
        crsctl unset css <parameter> - sets the Cluster Synchronization Services
parameter to its default
        crsctl query css votedisk - lists the voting disks used by Cluster
Synchronization Services
        crsctl add css votedisk <path> - adds a new voting disk
        crsctl delete css votedisk <path> - removes a voting disk
        crsctl enable crs - enables startup for all Oracle Clusterware daemons
        crsctl disable crs - disables startup for all Oracle Clusterware daemons
        crsctl start crs [-wait] - starts all Oracle Clusterware daemons
        crsctl stop crs [-wait] - stops all Oracle Clusterware daemons. Stops Oracle
Clusterware managed resources in case of cluster.
        crsctl start resources - starts Oracle Clusterware managed resources
        crsctl stop resources - stops Oracle Clusterware managed resources
        crsctl debug statedump css - dumps state info for Cluster Synchronization
Services objects
        crsctl debug statedump crs - dumps state info for Cluster Ready Services objects
        crsctl debug statedump evm - dumps state info for Event Manager objects
        crsctl debug log css [module:level] {,module:level} ... - turns on debugging for
Cluster Synchronization Services
        crsctl debug log crs [module:level] {,module:level} ... - turns on debugging for
Cluster Ready Services
        crsctl debug log evm [module:level] {,module:level} ... - turns on debugging for
Event Manager
        crsctl debug log res [resname:level] ... - turns on debugging for Event Manager
        crsctl debug trace css [module:level] {,module:level} ... - turns on debugging
for Cluster Synchronization Services
        crsctl debug trace crs [module:level] {,module:level} ... - turns on debugging
for Cluster Ready Services
        crsctl debug trace evm [module:level] {,module:level} ... - turns on debugging
for Event Manager
```

```
        crsctl query crs softwareversion [<nodename>] - lists the version of Oracle
Clusterware software installed
        crsctl query crs activeversion - lists the Oracle Clusterware operating version
        crsctl lsmodules css - lists the Cluster Synchronization Services modules that
can be used for debugging
        crsctl lsmodules crs - lists the Cluster Ready Services modules that can be used
for debugging
        crsctl lsmodules evm - lists the Event Manager modules that can be used for
debugging
If necessary any of these commands can be run with additional tracing by adding a
'trace'
 argument at the very front. Example: crsctl trace check css
```

The various *crsctl check* commands are very useful when resources do not start up, or the cluster is suffering from stability issues.

crsctl query css votedisk, *crsctl add css votedisk <path>*, and *crsctl delete css votedisk <path>* are useful when it is necessary to move the voting disk location. Remember that there may be no more than three copies of the voting disk.

Example:

```
[root@racnode1 bin]# crsctl add css votedisk /dev/sdg -force
```

 Tip: Arguably, some of the most useful commands are the *enable crs* and *disable crs* commands. When the *crsctl disable crs* command is run, the cluster will be disabled on startup. If any maintenance must be run on a cluster, this command is great to make sure no cluster components start on the system.

High Level Tools

Oracle's low level clusterware tools are great for digging into real issues or reconfiguring the cluster as a whole; however, there are several high level tools that are used for every day needs, such as:

- Listing cluster resources
- Starting and stopping cluster resources
- Relocating resources
- Registering and unregistering resources

- Enabling and disabling resources

Keep in mind that a resource is any part of the cluster system as a whole: VIP, GSD, ONS, ASM, the listener, the database, instances, and services.

crs_stat

crs_stat is probably the most commonly used of all Oracle RAC tools. This script accepts many different parameters to display information about all cluster resources.

By itself, the *crs_stat* command will list each resource registered with clusterware and show its status.

```
NAME=ora.racnode2.gsd
TYPE=application
TARGET=ONLINE
STATE=ONLINE on racnode2

NAME=ora.racnode2.ons
TYPE=application
TARGET=ONLINE
STATE=ONLINE on racnode2

NAME=ora.racnode2.vip
TYPE=application
TARGET=ONLINE
STATE=ONLINE on racnode2
```

Specifying the -t option will display information in tabular form. For instance:

```
[oracle@racnode1 ~]$ crs_stat -t
Name           Type         Target    State     Host
------------------------------------------------------------
ora.racdb.db   application  ONLINE    ONLINE    racnode2
ora....b1.inst application  ONLINE    ONLINE    racnode1
ora....b2.inst application  OFFLINE   OFFLINE
ora....SM1.asm application  ONLINE    ONLINE    racnode1
ora....E1.lsnr application  ONLINE    ONLINE    racnode1
ora....de1.gsd application  ONLINE    ONLINE    racnode1
ora....de1.ons application  ONLINE    ONLINE    racnode1
ora....de1.vip application  ONLINE    ONLINE    racnode1
ora....SM2.asm application  ONLINE    ONLINE    racnode2
ora....E2.lsnr application  ONLINE    ONLINE    racnode2
ora....de2.gsd application  ONLINE    ONLINE    racnode2
ora....de2.ons application  ONLINE    ONLINE    racnode2
```

```
ora....de2.vip application    ONLINE    ONLINE    racnode2
```

Another popular pair of options is a combination of -a and either -g or -r.

- -a allows a specific *resource_name* to be entered

- -g will return 0 if the resource is registered with clusterware, 1 if it is not

- -r will return 0 if the resource is running currently, and 1 if it is not

  - This can also be combined with -c *cluster_node* to narrow the query to a specific node

- Any of these commands are very useful in scripting

The *-p* option is also highly used as it prints the profile of any resource. This profile can be used to re-register resources later.

Other miscellaneous but useful options are:

- *-f* - Includes extended information and the profile

- *-ls* - Lists resources along with their owners and permissions

  - Can optionally include a *resource_name*

- *-v* - Returns extended information including failover counts

crs_start

crs_start is used to start resources, either one at a time or for the entire cluster.

To start all resources across a cluster, the *crs_start* command can be used with the -all option:

```
$ crs_start -all
```

To force a resource to start, all required prerequisites from that resource must be met. After that, the *crs_start* command can use the -f option to force startup. This is useful in cases like VIP failover, when the VIP must be relocated to another node.

If the -all option is not specified, a resource name must be given. For instance:

```
$ crs_start ora.racnode1.vip
```

 Tip: If one only wants to start a resource on a given node, the -c *node_name* option can be specified.

crs_stop

It would seem fairly obvious that *crs_stop* is exactly the opposite of *crs_start*. In fact, all of the options to *crs_stop* are identical to those of *crs_start*.

Please be aware that *crs_start* and *crs_stop* are precision tools; that is, they are used to start and stop a single resource in most cases. Usually using *srvctl* is the better option when starting and stopping resources.

crs_register

The *crs_register* utility can take profiles created with *crs_stat -p* or with *crs_profile* and register a resource with the cluster.

Profiles should be in the *CRS_HOME/crs/public* directory. The filename must be the name of the resource with an extension of .cap. For example, *ora.racnode2.vip* would be: *CRS_HOME/crs/public/ora.racnode2.vip.cap*.

Example of profile generation:

```
$ crs_stat -p ora.racnode2.vip >
    $ORA_CRS_HOME/crs/public/ora.racnode2.vip.cap
$ cat $ORA_CRS_HOME/crs/public/ora.racnode2.vip.cap
NAME=ora.racnode2.vip
TYPE=application
ACTION_SCRIPT=/u01/app/oracle/product/11.1.0/crs/bin/racgwrap
```

```
ACTIVE_PLACEMENT=1
AUTO_START=1
CHECK_INTERVAL=15
DESCRIPTION=CRS application for VIP on a node
FAILOVER_DELAY=0
FAILURE_INTERVAL=0
FAILURE_THRESHOLD=0
HOSTING_MEMBERS=racnode2
OPTIONAL_RESOURCES=
PLACEMENT=favored
REQUIRED_RESOURCES=
RESTART_ATTEMPTS=0
SCRIPT_TIMEOUT=60
START_TIMEOUT=0
STOP_TIMEOUT=0
UPTIME_THRESHOLD=7d
USR_ORA_ALERT_NAME=
USR_ORA_CHECK_TIMEOUT=0
USR_ORA_CONNECT_STR=/ as sysdba
USR_ORA_DEBUG=0
USR_ORA_DISCONNECT=false
USR_ORA_FLAGS=
USR_ORA_IF=eth0
USR_ORA_INST_NOT_SHUTDOWN=
USR_ORA_LANG=
USR_ORA_NETMASK=255.255.255.0
USR_ORA_OPEN_MODE=
USR_ORA_OPI=false
USR_ORA_PFILE=
USR_ORA_PRECONNECT=none
USR_ORA_SRV=
USR_ORA_START_TIMEOUT=0
USR_ORA_STOP_MODE=immediate
USR_ORA_STOP_TIMEOUT=0
USR_ORA_VIP=192.168.1.125
```

The simplest invocation of *crs_register* basically involves providing the resource name. Optionally, a directory can be provided where the .cap files will reside if they are not in the default location. For example:

```
$ crs_register ora.racnode2.vip -dir /u01/app/oracle/caps
```

A default registration would look like this:

```
$ crs_register ora.racnode2.vip
```

As long as a .cap file is present for that resource in the public location, it will become registered.

crs_unregister

The *crs_unregister* command simply unregisters a resource from the cluster.

 Tip: It is a good idea to save the profile or a resource before playing with this command!

To unregister a resource, run *crs_unregister* followed by the name of the resource. For example:

```
$ crs_unregister ora.racnode2.vip
```

srvctl

When it comes to RAC command line management, *srvctl* is the main attraction. This tool allows reconfiguration, addition, deletion, starting, stopping, and anything else involving management of RAC resources registered (or not registered) with the cluster.

Using this tool, it is possible to disable a database, or cause the system not to come online automatically, start and stop ASM, listeners, nodeapps, instances, and more.

To make all of this possible, there are a huge array of commands and options associated with *srvctl*. Thankfully, there is also help at every turn, with the -h option being available with every command or subcommand to show proper syntax. For instance, if someone is curious about commands to stop an Oracle instance:

```
$ srvctl
Usage: srvctl <command> <object> [<options>]
    command:
enable|disable|start|stop|relocate|status|add|remove|modify|getenv|setenv|un
setenv|config
    objects: database|instance|service|nodeapps|asm|listener
```

For detailed help on each command and object and its options use:

```
    srvctl <command> <object> -h

$ srvctl stop instance -h
Usage: srvctl stop instance -d <name> -i "<inst_name_list>" [-o
<stop_options>]
    -d <name>           Unique name for the database
    -i "<inst,...>"     Comma separated instance names
    -o <stop_options>   Options to shutdown command (e.g. normal,
transactional, immediate, or abort)
    -h                  Print usage
```

As this example shows, *srvctl* commands incorporate a main command, an object, and available options. This help text has shown that to stop an instance, the *stop* command, *instance* object, and -d and -i options will do the work:

```
$ srvctl stop instance -d racdb -i racdb1
```

Oracle uses the information registered within clusterware to know which node to use for the specified command.

Summary of srvctl Commands

- **add** - add nodeapps, databases, instances, ASM, or services

- **remove** - remove nodeapps, databases, instances, ASM, or services

- **config** - lists configuration for nodeapps, databases, ASM, or services

- **enable** - enables a database, instance, ASM, or services

- **disable** - disables a database, instances, ASM, or services

- **start** - start nodeapps, databases, instances, ASM, or services

- **stop** - stop nodeapps, databases, instances, ASM, or services

- **modify** - changes nodeapps, databases, instances, or services

- **relocate** - moves services between instances

- **status** - prints status of nodeapps, databases, instances, ASM, or services

- **getenv** - displays environment variables in the configuration of nodeapps, databases, instances, or services

- **setenv** - sets environment variables in the configuration of nodeapps, databases, instances, or services
- **unsetenv** - unsets environment variables in the configuration of nodeapps, databases, instances, or services

Starting and stopping services

It is very common to require a complete shutdown of all RAC services on a node and then post-maintenance to require them to all be brought back online. These commands will accomplish that task:

Stopping

```
$ srvctl stop instance -d db_name -i instance_name
$ srvctl stop asm -n node_name
$ srvctl stop nodeapps -n node_name
```

Starting

```
$ srvctl start nodeapps -n node_name
$ srvctl start asm -n node_name
$ srvctl start instance -d db_name -i instance_name
```

Changing the VIP IP address

Unfortunately, there are times when setup changes or some other requirement causes a DBA to have to reconfigure the cluster. One common change is the Virtual IP. If the public subnet changes or the IP addresses being used by the VIPs are required, the DBA may be required to migrate the VIPs to another node.

In order to do this, *srvctl* will be used heavily.

1. Stop all services and disable nodeapps:

   ```
   srvctl stop database -d db_name
   srvctl stop asm -n node_name1
   srvctl stop asm -n node_name2
   ```

2. Repeat for all nodes of the cluster

   ```
   srvctl stop nodeapps -n node_name1, node_name2,...
   srvctl disable nodeapps -n node_name1
   srvctl disable nodeapps -n node_name2
   ```

3. Make any necessary network changes and restart the network if needed.

4. If the public subnet or interface has changed, use the OIFCFG tool to change the public information.

5. As root, use *srvctl* to change the IP information in the OCR

```
srvctl modify nodeapps -n node_name1 -A IP_ADDRESS/NETMASK/IF_NAME
```

   - An example value for the -A flag would be: 192.168.1.135/255.255.255.0/eth0

   - Do this with the proper IP and node name for each node.

6. If the listener uses the VIP IP instead of hostname, modify the *listener.ora* on each node.

7. Start all services:

```
srvctl start nodeapps -n node_name1
srvctl start nodeapps -n node_name2
srvctl start asm -n node_name1
srvctl start asm -n node_name2
srvctl start database -d db_name
srvctl enable nodeapps -n node_name1
srvctl enable nodeapps -n node_name2
```

Adding or Removing Services

With Oracle 11g, the ability to perform service maintenance in DBCA is gone. As such, one of the best places to do so is at the command line with *srvctl*.

Srvctl allows services to be added for connections across the RAC cluster. With srvctl, a preferred and available list of nodes can be specified per service along with a TAF policy for failover.

The command follows the following syntax:

```
srvctl add service -d db_name -s service_name -r preferred_list [-a
available_list] [-P TAF_policy]
```

For example, create a service called BATCH that will run on node 3, but be available on node 2 in case of failure. This service will use the BASIC TAF policy as opposed to NONE or PRECONNECT.

```
$ srvctl add service -d racdb -s batch -r racnode3 -a racnode2 -P Basic
```

This service can be changed later with the -u option:

```
$ srvctl add service -d racdb -s batch -u -r racnode2,racnode3 -a racnode1
```

Likewise, a service can be removed with the *remove* command:

```
$ srvctl remove service -d racdb -s batch
```

If necessary, the -f option can be set to force remove a service. The -i option can also be set to indicate a specific instance to be removed from the service.

Conclusion

There are a great many tools included with Oracle RAC. Standard Oracle administrative tools have been grown to incorporate RAC as was seen at the beginning of the chapter. In addition, there is a suite of very powerful command line tools that can be used to manage every aspect of a RAC environment.

Using a combination of these tools, there is nothing a DBA cannot accomplish in the RAC environment. Because these tools aid in everything from backup and recovery to debugging to provisioning, a DBA must become proficient in their use in order to keep up with the needs of a clustered Oracle environment.

Oracle RAC Backup and Recovery

Backup and Recovery

One common misconception about Oracle RAC is that it provides all the backup necessary because multiple nodes are in use. However, it is important to remember that this redundancy is only at the instance level, not the database level. This means that if a failure occurs at the database level, such as lost or corrupt datafiles, RAC will not be able to keep the system online by itself.

There are two types of failure that must be considered:

- **Database Failure** is caused by a loss or corruption at the file level. Remember that while instances are redundant, database files are not.

- **Instance Failure** is caused when an instance crashes. In a RAC environment, the other instances in the cluster can continue to work, and the instance will recover itself when the system comes back online.

RAC Backup and Recovery

While RAC is a complex system involving multiple machines plugging into a centralized database, backup of the environment is relatively simple. The same basic tools or commands that are used to backup a single instance database can, in most cases, back up a RAC database.

A RAC database has one single set of datafiles and control files with redo log groups for each instance. All of these files are centralized, as RAC requires shared storage in order to run. Backing up those centralized files is the same as backing up files for a single instance, except that there will be a few more files.

A DBA can use many methods to backup his RAC database. These methods include:

- Logical export via *exp* or the Datapump tool *expdp*

- User-created cold or hot backups

- RMAN backups (hot or cold)

Before these backup options can be explored, it is important to understand how RAC and backups come together to form a complete redundancy solution.

Maximum Availability Architecture (MAA)

Oracle recommends a standard known as the Maximum Availability Architecture, or MAA. This plan provides contingencies both at the instance level and the database level.

High Availability (HA)

Generally speaking, instance level redundancy is known as High Availability (HA). This means that if an instance is lost in a RAC cluster, the high availability features ensure that other instances will take over the workload as seamlessly as possible. HA does not cover datafile loss or corruption. Instead, it only covers the runtime components of the Oracle environment.

High availability can be achieved in a RAC environment when proper failover techniques are used, such as Transparent Application Failover (TAF) and/or Fast Connect Failover (FCF). Though an instance failure will require reconfiguration, i.e. instance recovery of the lost instance, the basic components of RAC should still be available.

Disaster Recovery (DR)

Disaster Recovery is necessary in the case of datafile or environment loss and corruption. If the centralized database files, the central storage array, or the entire server environment is lost, recovery will be necessary.

A loss of datafiles is relatively easy to recover compared to a full server environment loss. Using RMAN, a backup can be used to restore and recover missing or corrupt datafiles. If the affected tablespaces are not the SYSTEM, SYSAUX, or UNDO tablespaces, the rest of the database can even stay online while the recovery is in progress.

However, when an entire environment such as a server room or office building is lost, as in a natural disaster, disaster recovery is required. Disaster recovery involves having a duplicated database environment in another location, preferably one outside of the same range of natural disasters that could occur at the primary site. For instance, if the primary database cluster is in Florida, it is a good idea to place the disaster recovery (standby) site in a location without hurricanes.

The primary Oracle tool for disaster recovery is Data Guard; however, there are many third party options also offered to achieve a full disaster recovery implementation.

Whatever tool is used, it is important that it make incremental updates to the standby environment as much as possible in order to be available in the case of a failure. It is important to calculate beforehand what the maximum allowable downtime will be. This is usually decided by management as a company's service level agreements (SLA) will be affected by this downtime.

Physical Backups

Physical backups are created by duplicating the actual files that comprise the database. These files include the datafiles, control files, and redo/archive logs. Additionally, the SPFILE can be considered a crucial database file.

Hot Backups

Backups can be taken while the database is either online or offline. In order to take online backups, the database must be in hot backup mode.

 Remember that in a RAC environment, even if only one instance of many is online in OPEN mode, the database is considered to be 'online'.

When a hot backup is taken, the files in the backup are necessarily inconsistent. By themselves they are not able to fix a broken database. With archive logs, however, the backup files can be caught up allowing full recovery to the point of time of failure in the case of a crash. The database is fully available while in hot backup mode, but Oracle performs internal block activity to prevent what are known as fractured blocks.

Cold Backups

It is also possible to take a cold backup. This is a backup that is taken when the entire database environment is offline. In the case of a RAC environment, this means that all nodes must be in an offline state such as shut down, nomount, or mount.

A cold backup does not require any archive logs in order to be immediately usable as a recovery option. The backup itself is consistent, meaning it can be restored and opened immediately. However, without archive logs it will be impossible to recover the database to the point in time at which the failure occurred. In a hot backup, archive logs are both the glue which brings the inconsistent datafiles together and the mechanism by which the database can be brought up to date. In a cold backup, archive logs are only used to bring the database up to date.

It is important to remember that a cold backup requires the entire database be offline. As such, cold backups are not necessarily popular in the RAC world, as the purpose of RAC is to maintain 24 x 7 availability.

Restore and Recover

The previous two sections on hot and cold backups made frequent use of the words restore and recover. In backup and recovery, restoring is performed when files are placed back in their proper locations by either overwriting corrupt files or replacing missing files. Recovery, on the other hand, is bringing those files up-to-date to ensure complete database consistency. This is accomplished by catching up all datafiles to the same SCN.

Logical Backups

Logical backups involve backing up the data contained within the database, but not the physical database files. The most popular form of logical backup is performed with Oracle's export utilities. These include the *exp* command for 9i and lower compatible dumps, and the *expdp* command for the 10g datapump dumps.

If a database is in use when a logical backup is being taken, then the backup will be inconsistent. Though there are mechanisms by which an online logical dump can be created with full consistency, they are costly since they require enough UNDO to satisfy the entire time in which the logical dump occurs.

Usually a logical backup will be taken at the schema or table level to quickly dump tables to physical files in case the data is quickly needed again. This is different from a physical backup where the entire datafile or database must be recovered in order to restore a single table.

Creating Backups in a RAC Environment

There are several tools included within Oracle to achieve all backup methodologies. These tools include:

- User-created scripts
- exp and expdp
- RMAN

Additionally, it is possible to implement user-created scripts to perform a backup.

Using Scripts for Backup

A cold backup can be taken on a RAC database whether it is in ARCHIVELOG mode or not. Cold backups require that the entire database environment be shut down; this includes access by all instances in the cluster.

Once the database is completely shut down on all nodes, a script can be used to copy all datafiles, redo logs, control files, the SPFILE, and archive logs to a remote location. Careful documentation should exist recording where these files must be placed in order to restore the database in the event of a failure.

Information about current file placement can be found with the following queries:

```
select file_name from dba_data_files;

select name from v$controlfile;

select member from v$logfile;

select value from v$parameter where name = 'spfile';
```

All files returned by these scripts must be backed up in order for a cold backup to be complete consistent.

In the case of a hot backup or a cold backup from which the database will be fully recovered, archive logs must also be backed up. In order to become fully consistent, all archive logs during which a hot backup took place and all archive logs up to the point of recovery must be identified. The *v$archived_log* view shows archive logs for all instances.

 Even though gv$ views are usually used to display RAC information instead of traditional v$ views, in the case of redo and archive logs the information regarding all nodes is stored on each node. Instead of specifically using *inst_id* as most gv$ views do, the thread# keeps track of the instance to which each redo or archive log belongs.

The biggest drawback to using script driven backups is management. When using RMAN (Recovery Manager), Oracle's internal dictionary will keep track of backups within the control file or an external catalog. When using user-made scripts, there is no record of backups taken or locations within Oracle. All backup information must be documented very carefully.

Cold backups present another major drawback. The database must be down while the backup takes place. Again, in a RAC environment this defeats the purpose of high availability.

Hot backups, while better on uptime, do cause issues when run from user-created scripts. In order to prevent block fracturing, the DBA must place each datafile in hot backup mode. This is done either at the database level or the datafile level:

- Datafile hot backup mode:
  ```
  alter datafile '/path/to/datafile.dbf' begin backup;
  ```

- Database hot backup mode:
  ```
  alter database begin backup;
  ```

Once the backup is complete, the files can be taken out of hot backup mode:

- Datafile hot backup mode:

```
alter datafile '/path/to/datafile.dbf' end backup;
```

- Database hot backup mode:

```
alter database end backup;
```

When a datafile is in hot backup mode via these commands, Oracle must record the entire contents of a data block to redo the first time that block is modified since going into hot backup mode.

For instance, if file #5 is placed in hot backup mode and someone writes data to block #50 via DDL or DML, the entire contents of the data block will be written to redo logs. After the initial change to block #50, writes to the block will only require the deltas be recorded to redo. If the database block size is the default of 8k, this will result in a large amount of data being written to redo if the database is in use during the hot backup.

While it may be tempting to try taking a backup without placing the datafiles into hot backup mode, it is obviously not recommended. The backup will likely not be usable and will not be supported by Oracle. Even if third party snapshot tools are used, it is necessary to place the datafiles into hot backup mode before taking the snapshot. Once the snapshot is complete, the files can be taken out of hot backup mode.

If manual scripts are going to be used, it is a good idea to generate these scripts using the views mentioned in this section to automatically create the backup script required. This ensures that when database changes are made, such as the addition of a datafile, the changes will be present during the next backup.

Exporting Logical Data

The preferred method for exporting logical data in Oracle 11g is the Datapump Export utility (*expdp*). This utility is able to write tables, schemas, or the full database to flat files on disk. These files can be moved and imported into other databases.

Exports are not a valid solution for a real backup methodology. While effective for quick snaps of data or as a last resort option, only a physical backup can be guaranteed to be recoverable in the event of a failure. Many shops perform three phases of backup:

- Data Guard to standby environment

- RMAN backups locally, copied to tape

- Export dumps taken as a last resort

This ensures redundancy at every level. Although the export is not useful for a full recovery, it can still be useful if all else is lost.

RMAN Backups

Oracle 9i and 10g greatly improved the interface for RMAN, making it easier for any DBA to take backups as necessary. Oracle 11g allows for fast and easy backups in RMAN, simplifying backup management and recovery.

Conclusion

Types of failure and the programs needed for recovery have been explained in this chapter, including physical and logical backups. It is important to note the difference between database and instance failure and to have the proper tools to prevent total loss of data. How to create backups in a RAC environment is also covered.

RAC in the Enterprise

Executive Summary

RAC (Real Application Clusters) provides businesses with some outstanding benefits. Not only is nearly 100% uptime possible, but scalability is possible using lower priced hardware.

These things come with a cost: increased licensing cost, training, consultants, software, hardware, and other components of a RAC system. In addition, RAC only provides support for part of the availability spectrum. Other costs will have to be endured to provide a Maximum Availability Architecture (MAA).

It is important for managers to understand these concepts before embarking on the RAC quest; remember that although one's employees are hopefully top notch and know what they are doing, it is the manager's credibility if one jumps into a project without having a full view of its possible repercussions.

What is RAC?

In many ways, RAC seems too good to be true. RAC offers 24 x 7 database availability, true scalability, and high performance all on low cost commodity servers.

The Oracle System

The Oracle system is formed of two parts: the database and the instance.

Component 1: The Database

The database is simply the files on disk. An Oracle database consists of three specific required file types:

- Datafiles
- Control Files
- Redo Logs

Datafiles

Oracle datafiles are the final storage location of the data. All data that is inserted, updated, or deleted will make its way to the datafiles once the change is committed. These files are physically stored on disk resources.

Datafiles are grouped into tablespaces. A tablespace is a logical disk area that Oracle objects (tables and indexes) can be stored in. When a user creates an object, the object is placed logically in the tablespace and physically in the data file.

In Oracle 11g, there are two tablespaces that are required: the SYSTEM and SYSAUX tablespaces.

Control Files

The control file is the record keeper of the Oracle Database. It keeps track of the current state of the datafiles and redo logs, archive logs, and the database. Multiplexing the control file is highly recommended.

The control file is a required file on non-RAC and RAC systems. Losing a control file will cause an instance crash.

Redo Logs

Redo logs act like a tape recorder that records every change in the Oracle database. As changes occur, they are regularly recorded in the online redo logs.

Oracle can replay the saved transactions in the redo logs and re-apply lost transactions back into the database. Many times, this means that Oracle can recover from a crash without the DBA having to do anything other than just telling the database to start up.

At a minimum, Oracle requires two redo logs. Oracle will write redo to the first log and when the first log is full, Oracle will switch to the second log and write the same redo. Each of these individual online redo logs is known as an online redo log group.

Like control files, it is a good idea to have multiplexed copies of the online redo files in each group. Also like control files, it is a good idea to have multiplexed copies of the redo logs. Each copy of the redo log file within a log group is called a redo log member. Each redo log group can have one or more members.

Component 2: The Instance

The Oracle Instance is the runtime component of Oracle. The instance is made up of the following parts:

- Binary Processes
- RAM

Binary Processes

Oracle runs five critical binary processes that are activated when the instance is started.

- **SMON** – The System Monitor. SMON is primarily used to recover a crashed instance.

- **PMON** – The Process Monitor. PMON cleans up dead processes and registers network services for the instance.

- **DBWR** – Database Writer. DBWR is used to write blocks to datafiles (transition from instance to database).

- **LGWR** – Log Writer. LGWR writes redo information to the redo log files.

- **CKPT** – Checkpoint. CKPT assists in keeping all files in sync.

If any of these processes fail, the entire instance of Oracle crashes. In a single instance environment, this results in downtime.

Note that on Microsoft Windows, these five processes are threaded under a single process called ORACLE.EXE.

RAM

Oracle stores data in RAM in an area called the System Global Area (SGA). The SGA is broken down into pools where data can be temporarily stored before being discarded, overwritten, or flushed to disk. These pools or memory areas are:

- **Buffer Cache** – Stores cached blocks of data from Oracle datafiles when queried. Also stores data written with inserts, updates, and deletes called Data Manipulation Language, or DML. Data is flushed from this pool via DBWR to the datafiles. The buffer cache is very important to RAC.

- **Shared Pool** – Caches the means by which SQL can be executed, called an execution plan. When SQL is run, it must be parsed; if the execution plan is cached in the shared pool, the parse phase is sped up considerably.

- **Log Buffer** – Stores change data to be flushed to the current redo log file. Flushing occurs every commit, every three seconds, when the buffer is one third full, when it reaches 1MB, on checkpoint, or when required by DBWR.

Cache Fusion

RAC provides a multiple instance, single database system. In a RAC environment, there is one shared set of datafiles. Each instance in the cluster will have its SGA (RAM area) and binary processes. Control files

---

and redo log files will belong to each instance but will reside on shared disk for recovery purposes.

A RAC environment uses cache fusion to bring all the instances in the cluster together. Each instance has its own buffer cache. Oracle fuses these caches together into a single global buffer cache. This occurs over a private network called a private or cluster interconnect. The cluster interconnect allows each node of the RAC cluster to share cached data located in the buffer cache with any other node on the cluster.

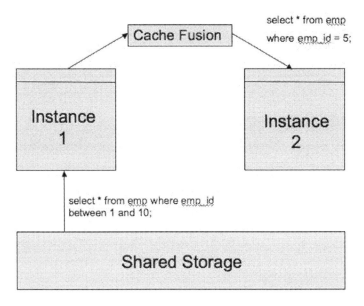

Figure 7.1: *A Simple View of Cache Fusion at Work*

Instance 1 (server 1) queries the centralized storage to find all employees between 1 and 10. Once this query has been executed and fetched, the data will be cached in Instance 1's buffer cache. If Instance 1 were to require any of this data again, it would have to look no further than local RAM. RAM is much faster than disk, so the query would return much quicker.

Again, in Figure 7.1, suppose Instance 2 runs a query that wants a row that Instance 1 already has cached. In this case, Instance 2 would receive the data over the high-speed network interconnect using cache fusion. This RAM-to-RAM transfer over the network is not as fast as local RAM, but it definitely beats going to disk.

High Availability

RAC also provides the benefit of High Availability. If Instance 2 (Figure 7.1) crashes, Instance 1 will take over the user load. All connections that would have pointed to Instance 2 will fail over to Instance 1. In some cases, connections that were already pointing at Instance 2 will also fail over.

Uptime

The primary goal of RAC can be summed up in a single word: Uptime. Data drives business. Applications, DSS, expert systems, reporting, analytics - they all require a steady stream of data to keep them alive.

If a bank loses its core transaction database for even a single hour, it can cause massive amounts of error, possible data corruption and millions of dollars lost.

Oracle RAC is a High Availability (HA) system. It makes downtime more bearable by providing connection to multiple nodes. If, in a four-node RAC cluster, a single node crashes, three nodes will take over immediately without a single second of downtime.

Unplanned Downtime

Unplanned downtime can last from seconds to hours in extreme situations and can happen because of some of the most simple or unexpected issues.

Examples of events causing unplanned downtime:

- Power failure

- Overheated server room

- Flooding in server room

- Kernel panic

- Fat fingered mistake (for instance, a systems administrator kills a required process such as SMON)

- Oracle Internal errors

- Hackers

Planned Downtime

Planned downtime is more graceful than unplanned, of course, but in some ways can be worse than unplanned downtime. Depending on the software on the server, it could require frequent restarts in order to keep things updated. Some developers and administrators want daily maintenance periods which can cause planned downtime to be the bulk of the total downtime.

RAC alleviates these issues by allowing a single server to be down while the other RAC server(s) keep processing. Work can progress in a rolling fashion where one server at a time comes down, thereby allowing the database to always remain online.

Scalability

There are two ways to scale hardware: vertically and horizontally. Vertical scaling means to build up. Add CPUs, RAM, and such until the system is full. To visualize scaling vertically, think of Manhattan. There is no more room on the horizontal plane. There is no room to build new buildings. However, adding new stories to existing buildings is possible. This is scaling up.

Scaling horizontally is the practice of adding new systems to the cluster. In an area with ample open land, when new developments are needed, building taller buildings is unnecessary. Building out is more practical, scaling upon the horizontal plane.

Oracle, vendors, and consultants may mention that RAC is good because of the price. At first glance, it seems expensive because of the added cost per CPU on top of what is already being paid for Oracle. However, it can actually decrease costs by decreasing hardware requirements.

RAC allows the use of multiple low cost machines together in order to provide the same capability of a single large system with the added benefit of high availability. For instance, four 16-CPU systems instead of a single 64-CPU server could be used. Now new servers can be added as needed.

In addition, a single system may have underutilized resources. If the system is waiting on a RAM resource, but the CPUs are at only 50% capacity, half of the CPUs are wasted. In a RAC environment, every server can be utilized to the max. The concurrent processes will be balanced across all the nodes of the cluster, and will therefore have a better chance to use otherwise unclaimed resources.

The addition of an instance creates the opportunity to support a larger number of concurrent users. Any instance introduced into the RAC system opens up new memory buffers and permits more user connections without affecting the performance of the other instances.

A RAC database system provides excellent scalability options for the users. As the need arises, DBAs can expand or add the number of nodes in the cluster. This enhances the total database engine computing power when the need for high performance arises. With the additional nodes and instances in the database cluster, the system is able to accommodate demands. Consider the following statements

- If the application will scale by adding RAM and CPUs, it should scale on RAC.

- If the application will not scale by adding RAM and CPUs, it typically will not scale on RAC.

- RAC can expose application design issues that were not exposed on a single instance non-RAC system.

- A poorly designed application could work fine on a non-RAC single instance but might not work very well on RAC.

When one thinks about database scalability on RAC, one needs to visualize the data blocks. Constantly having to ship a large number of the same data blocks back and forth via cache fusion may not be scalable.

Bert Scalzo, Ph.D has a great document online called "RAC Be Nimble RAC Be Quick." The image below originates from his document. Remember, the application should be built so that an instance can run full throttle without worrying what the other instances are doing. Oracle RAC can provide near linear scalability.

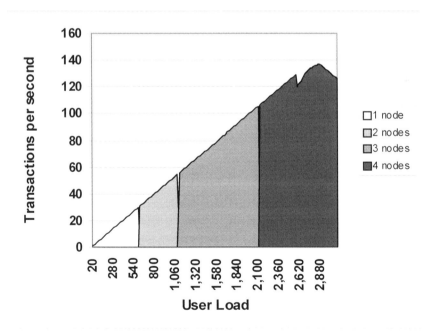

Figure 7.2: *Multi-node Capability of RAC (Source: Bert Scalzo)*

Implementation

RAC is a complex system to implement. In the authors' experience, most companies require a consultant to come in to help plan the move to RAC and for the actual installation itself. There are many different pieces to the RAC environment from networking to disk drives to clusterware to Oracle itself. On top of that, there are some costly disk requirements.

In order to implement a RAC system, a shared storage device is required. A single instance database can use Direct Attached Storage (DAS), which is an array of inexpensive disks connected to a single server. A SAN (Storage Area Network) is much more expensive and is capable of connecting to many servers, usually through fibre-channel connections. This requires a unique set of hardware ranging from Host Bus Adapters (HBA), a fabric switch, to the SAN itself, and it can get very costly.

Redundancy can also be costly. Most administrators require redundancy within each server as well. This means doubling up on hardware, and doubling the hardware equals double the cost. For example, multiple Host Bus Adapters, multiple network cards, multiple power sources and more can be required. The multiple HBA cards are used in case a single one fails, but this usually requires expensive software to manage.

Another cost is the network connection. The RAC system requires a cluster interconnect in order to accommodate RAM-to-RAM transfers of data blocks. This interconnect must be very fast, high bandwidth with low latency. Interconnects, such as InfiniBand and Myrinet, can accommodate this but are very expensive. Though RAC does provide horizontal scalability, if the cluster interconnect cannot handle the traffic, extra servers will actually degrade performance instead of helping it. The only way around this issue is to change the entire application to accommodate RAC, or purchase other means of disk storage such as Solid State Disk.

Learning Curve

There is a definite learning curve when it comes to RAC. Because of all the different components that make up a RAC environment, multiple levels of training may be required.

System Administrators will have to learn how to work with the disk resources. Complex SAN environments such as EMC and NetApp can require training of their own. In addition, Oracle RAC will only function when using specific disk setups such as ASM, OCFS, or a 3rd Party CFS, and the administrator will have to assist in setup. Setting up and administering the hardware is no small task!

Network Administrators will have to learn how to work with the new interconnect. If a specialized interconnect such as InfiniBand is used, training and consulting may be required.

Of all the staff, DBAs will have the greatest learning curve. They will have to understand how to set up and administer clusterware, volume manager or the file system of choice, the RAC specific features of Oracle, and troubleshooting for clusters. While this does not sound like much, it makes up many days of training, lots of trial and error, and even a little bit of "miracle work" at times.

As the manager, one may require training to deal with setting up training sessions, consulting, and dealing with employees with some great new marks on their resumes!

RAC is Transparent to Users, not the DBA

From an end user's perspective, a RAC system behaves much like a normal database. Oracle's goal is to provide transparency for all users so no one ever knows they are even touching a complex RAC environment.

However, this does not apply to the DBA. The DBA must keep everything in the RAC environment monitored, up-to-date, and running perfectly. With so many components, it is possible for more things to go wrong.

The DBA must monitor the cluster, the shared disk setup, ASM or OCFS if they are in use, the database, all instances, listeners, and more in-depth metrics such as cache coherency, interconnect latency, disk times from multiple systems, and many other things. Although tools such as Grid Control help perform this monitoring, it costs more money, requires more implementation, and possibly even training and consulting.

Remember also that humans are fast becoming the most expensive part of the IT environment. DBAs that are RAC proficient are usually better paid. In addition, more DBAs may be needed to keep everything running smoothly.

Another note on usage comes from the architecture of RAC as a whole. Remember the cache fusion component that was covered in the last section? Well, it is nice, but it is not always a surefire winner. While RAM-to-RAM transfers over the network are indeed faster than reading from disk, they are still not as fast as a local RAM read. Key queries that used to be lightning fast may slow down. This is caused by the application pointing at multiple nodes in the cluster.

In addition, the interconnect MUST be very fast with low latency in order to sustain the RAC cluster. If the interconnect is bogged down with too many nodes, performance could hit rock bottom. RAC is scalable, and it performs well, but it is not the end–all, be- all of performance. In fact, most database professionals find it easier to tune a single instance system than a RAC environment due to the lower level of complexity and resources required for management.

Maximum Availability Architecture (MAA)

RAC protects against instance and server failure by providing multiple servers with which one can be connected. However, remember that all data will be in centralized storage. There is still a possibility of data failure or data center loss.

Data failure is the worst of the three that have been seen thus far (instance and system failure), resulting in the loss or corruption of data. Some disk failures are non-disastrous; for instance, if a disk is mirrored with hardware or software RAID. Even then, if excessive disks are lost, it is possible that production data could be lost as well, thereby requiring some form of recovery. User error can also cause data loss if an operating system user removes database files with a command such as *rm*. In this case, the file will be removed, and the disk mirror will provide no protection. Lastly, corruption can occur if hardware or software bugs result in inappropriate data being written to the datafiles.

Data center loss occurs when a system is completely lost, usually as the result of some sort of natural disaster. A hurricane, flood, or tornado may destroy or seriously disable an entire data center resulting in a combined loss of servers and disk. This is by far the worst unplanned-downtime scenario and can only be protected against with extensive, and usually expensive, disaster recovery methods.

Oracle provides many options for preventing downtime and data loss, all of which make up the Maximum Availability Architecture (MAA). The MAA provides redundancy on all components and employs different Oracle tools. RAC only makes up one piece of the MAA; it does not take into account all possible problems.

These tools, as recently mentioned, must provide protection for planned and unplanned downtime. They must also protect against varying levels of unplanned downtime ranging from single server outages, which RAC covers, to entire data center loss, which RAC does not cover.

Some businesses choose not to follow all the guidelines for maximum availability. When considering a high availability strategy, the DBA must consider:

- Recovery Time Objective (RTO)

- Recovery Point Objective (RPO)

- Downtime Cost-per-Minute

- Available Resources

The RTO defines the allowable downtime for the database. An advertising company may allow hours of downtime; however, a bank will usually allow no downtime whatsoever. RPO defines the allowable data loss if a failure occurs. If batch processes load the data, it may be that hours or even days of data could be reloaded. However, for a system that allows direct access by the end user, such as an online store or ATM machine, zero data loss is allowed.

Downtime can be expensive. Depending on the system, costs can range from dollars per minute to tens of thousands of dollars lost for every minute the database is unavailable. However, uptime is expensive as well. It has been shown how costly RAC can be for a business. Now it can be seen that even more may be required for a fully bulletproof system.

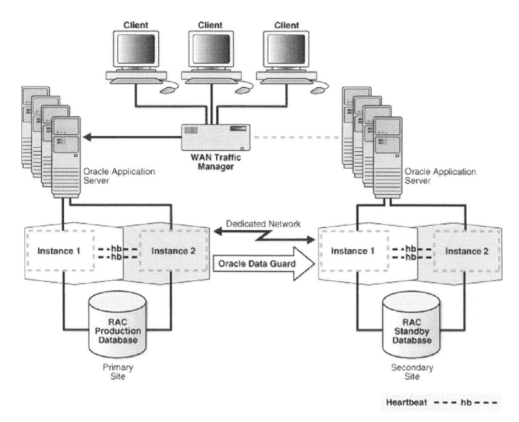

Figure 7.3: *Example of an HA Configuration using MAA Best Practices*

Many other HA solutions require the backup server to sit uselessly idle. A solid HA solution like Oracle 11g RAC is good for the users, management, System Administrators and DBAs.

With multiple instances, the RAC system gives a near zero failure environment. Even when one or more nodes fail in the cluster, for whatever reason, as long as there is one instance running, the database resources are provided.

With the help of the transparent application failover (TAF) configuration, operations are transferred automatically to the surviving instance.

Users will appreciate the ability to always connect to their apps even when a server node experiences a total hardware or instance failure. Management and the other System Administrators are happy when the users are happy. Then the DBA can sleep more soundly and work a more balanced 9 – 5 schedule. A DBA can now take a node offline knowing the other nodes will prevent the users from noticing.

The major benefits of the RAC database system are scalability and high availability. No business operations can run without the use of database resources. That is why the geeks, and more specifically, the DBAs shall inherit the earth.

Deployment Considerations

The RAC database provides the technology of cache fusion, which simplifies application deployment issues. Before cache fusion had been fully implemented, many of the applications had to selectively access the multiple instances in a way that would not result in update contentions, thereby minimizing pings and false pings. With the full implementation of cache fusion, many types of applications are able to connect and use the multiple RAC instances while avoiding the performance issues that result from cross instance updates. There are two broad types of data access methodologies:

- **OLTP:** Traditionally, online transaction processing (OLTP) users access the database resources or data blocks randomly. The transaction life, or access duration, is usually very short. With this method, there is limited conflict or contention with the data sets.

- **DSS:** Decision support systems (DSS) and data warehousing (DW) applications focus more on analysis of the data and the creation of various reports. A data warehouse is a relational database that is designed for analysis rather than transaction processing. A data warehouse usually contains historical data that is derived from transaction data as well as from other sources. The warehouse separates the analysis workload from transaction workloads and consolidates data from several sources.

Using tools such as online analytical processing (OLAP) extraction engines or other statistical tools, large data sets are processed. With this method, for any given query a large number of data blocks are read and analyzed. Performance is a crucial factor with this type of access.

The OLTP and DW databases have traditionally been separated into different servers and instances. The data warehouse is updated or refreshed by loading data from the OLTP on an appropriate schedule. Data warehouses typically use an extract, transport, transform, and load (ETL) process, which involves complex and time-consuming steps such as data exports and network copies. The mixed OLTP and DW databases used to compete often for resources, resulting in update contentions. This created performance issues.

With multiple instances, the RAC database is in a perfect position to segregate the activity on different nodes while still maintaining single database storage. This not only results in better performance levels for both types of data activities, OLTP and DSS, but also gives administrative flexibility and cost savings.

Database Consolidation

The main purpose of database consolidation is to reduce cost. Today, when so many software choices are supposedly free, DBAs see the number of MySQL and PostgreSQL installations growing. However, Oracle continues to dominant in the area of Enterprise Applications. LAMP (Linux, Apache, MySQL, and PHP) development is growing, but many Enterprise level applications, in the authors' experience, do not support MySQL or PostgreSQL.

For 2007, Fortune magazine ranks Oracle Corporation as the sixth (6th) most profitable technology company, making $4.3 billion. Google came in seventh (7th) place. MySQL and PostgreSQL have a long climb ahead of them before they are major players in the Enterprise Application market.

As CTOs are forced to cut costs, one trend is to consolidate databases and use Oracle Standard Edition where the features of Oracle Enterprise

Edition are not needed. This could be called license scale-down. The cost savings of using Standard Edition in place of Enterprise Edition can be significant. It is important to understand what features and options are only available to Enterprise Edition

Features and Options Only Available to Oracle 11g Enterprise Edition

Here is a list of the features and options that can be found in the Oracle 11g Enterprise Edition. This gives the manager an idea of what features best fit the needs of his/her company and can help in deciding whether the Enterprise Edition or the Standard Edition is the best choice for the company's needs.

- Oracle Data Guard
    - Redo Apply, SQL Apply, Snapshot Standby, Network Compression, Active Data Guard
- Rolling upgrades
- Fast-start selectable recovery time
- Online schema reorganization
- Flashback
    - Table, Database, Transaction, Transaction Query, Data Archive
- Block-level media recovery
- Block change tracking for faster incremental backups
- Parallel backup and recovery
- Fast RMAN Compression (ZLIB)
- Point-in-time tablespace recovery
- Trial recovery
- Oracle Advanced and Label Security
- Virtual Private Database

- Fine grained auditing
- New results cache feature
- New Client Side Query Cache
- Change Management and Configuration Management Packs
- Diagnostic and Tuning Packs
- Duplexed backup sets
- Resource Manager
- SQL Plan Management
- Partitioning
- Data Mining
- Direct Load and OLTP Compression
- Bitmapped index and bitmapped join index
- Various Parallel operations
  - Query, Statistics gathering, Index build, Index scan, Data Pump, Export/Import
- Data Pump Compression
- Export Transportable tablespace
- Materialized View Query Rewrite
- Asynchronous Change Data Capture
- Full Oracle Streams options
- Messaging Gateway
- Advanced Replication
- Connection Manager
- InfiniBand Support
- Oracle Spatial

Features and Options available to Oracle 11g Standard Edition

Here is a list of the features and options for the Standard Edition so that the manager has a comparison with the Enterprise Edition.

- Basic Standby Database (Manually managed)
- Online system changes
- Flashback Query
- Online Backup and Recovery
- Incremental Backup and Recovery
- Default RMAN Compression (BZIP2)
- Oracle Fail Safe (Windows only)
- Data Recovery Advisor
- Transparent Application Failover
- Real Application Clusters
- Oracle Clusterware
- Automatic Workload Management
- Encryption toolkit
- Java support
- Database Web services
- SQLJ
- JDBC drivers
- XML support in the database
- Xquery
- Objects and extensibility
- Various PL/SQL features

- - Regular Expressions, Stored procedures, Triggers, Server pages, native compile
- Java Server Pages and Java native compilation
- Various Microsoft items
  - Developer Tools for Visual Studio .Net, DTC support, Active Directory integration, ODP.Net, .Net stored procedures
- 64-bit Itanium support
- Globalization support
- Application Express
- SQL*Plus and SQL Developer
- Fast Lightweight Server Install
- Easy Client Install
- Oracle Enterprise Manager – Database Control
- Automatic
  - memory management, storage management, undo management, statistics management
- RMAN
- Backup to Flash Recovery Area
- Server generated Alerts
- Application Tracing
- Resumable Space Allocation
- SQL Analytic functions
- Function-based indexes
- Basic Data Pump Export/Import
- Import Transportable Tablespace
- Star query transformation (b-tree only)
- Sample scan

- Summary Management – Materialized View creation and refresh
- Direct Path Load API
- External tables
- SQL Model
- Synchronous Change Data Capture
- Oracle Streams Apply only
- Oracle Streams Advanced Queuing
- Basic Replication
- Distributed queries/transactions
- Job Scheduler
- External procedures
- Generic connectivity
- Transparent Gateways
- Connection polling
- Oracle Locator
- Oracle Workspace Manager
- MultiMedia
- Oracle Text
- SecureFiles
- Database event triggers
- Various column operations
  - drop, rename, constraint, virtual
- Amazing Invisible Indexes
- Index-organized table
- Instead-of triggers
- LOB support

- LogMiner

- Multiple block size support

- Temporary tables

That was a long list! This information might save one's company $50,000 in Oracle licensing costs. For larger sites, it could even save the company millions of dollars. The great thing about Oracle 11g Standard Edition is that it is easy to upgrade to Enterprise Edition when necessary.

Whether Standard Edition is an option or not, many enterprises are showing interest in major data or database consolidation. For example, dozens of instances residing on several hosts or servers are merged into a large database. With a powerful server platform, abundant memory, and ample processor resources, it is common to establish a very large database (VLDB) that can accumulate terabytes of data. This license can be called scale-in.

Oracle VLDB has proven to be a good cost saving solution. Oracle 11g Enterprise Edition offers dynamic parallel processing features that can offer significant performance time improvements. This approach provides:

- Reduced TCO in terms of licensing, staffing, and consulting fees

- Improved availability with the focus on fewer databases

- Higher security

- Centralized backup and archive

RAC with Grid is an ideal solution to take advantage of these developments. RAC supports VLDB databases for data consolidation and large data warehousing databases. Even in a packaged application environment, as in SAP or PeopleSoft, there is a tendency towards consolidating the databases to provide lower cost and better administrative flexibility.

With the power of processors today, reducing a corporation's database server footprint to be a tenth of what it was is a real possibility. Virtual machines are a big part of enterprise server consolidation efforts. Oracle VM is a less known product in the Virtual Machine marketplace but is interesting because it is fully supported for various Oracle products. See Metalink Doc 464754.1 for the latest information about RAC on Oracle VM.

Conclusion

Oracle RAC provides a scalable and highly available data storage platform. Multi-instances and multiple nodes make RAC a powerful database platform. Most applications can use this multi-node clustered database without any code modification. This chapter also listed the options and features for both Oracle 11g Standard Edition and Enterprise Edition that helps one make a decision on which package is ideal for one's situation.

References

Multiple Components in One Database - (MCOD) Presentation by George Leffers

BEA WebLogic Server and WebLogic Express Administration Guide

Supporting Siebel eBusiness Suites in an Oracle High Availability and Scalability Environment - James Qiu, Jianwen Lai, Anda Zhao - Oracle World Presentation

Metalink.com

Oracle.com

Database-11g-product-family-technical-whitepaper.pdf

Index

About Steve Karam

Steve Karam is one of the few DBAs worldwide to achieve both the Oracle 10g Certified Master certification and the Oracle ACE designation, both of which he received before the age of 26. As both a production DBA and an instructor, he has a proven track record in performance and troubleshooting on dozens of high profile Oracle systems including complex RAC environments. Additionally, Steve has been developing against Oracle databases for over twelve years on a variety of platforms including C, C++, Java, PHP, and Application Express.

Steve is also involved heavily in the Oracle community as the President of the Hampton Roads Oracle Users Group, Web Chair for the IOUG RAC SIG, and judge for the yearly Oracle Academy educational competition.

About Bryan Jones

Bryan Jones is an Oracle Certified Professional with 10+ years of hands-on Oracle experience. Currently Bryan works full-time as a Senior Lead Oracle DBA for a Top-Level Federal Government Office. He also assists Unisys DBAs and Federal Government DBAs with RDMBS performance tuning issues.

Bryan has a Bachelor of Science in Computer Science from Westminster College and a Masters in Computer Science from Creighton University.

About Mike Reed

When he first started drawing, Mike Reed drew just to amuse himself. It wasn't long, though, before he knew he wanted to be an artist. Today he does illustrations for children's books, magazines, catalogs, and ads.

He also teaches illustration at the College of Visual Art in St. Paul, Minnesota. Mike Reed says, "Making pictures is like acting — you can paint yourself into the action." He often paints on the computer, but he also draws in pen and ink and paints in acrylics. He feels that learning to draw well is the key to being a successful artist.

Mike is regarded as one of the nation's premier illustrators and is the creator of the popular "Flame Warriors" illustrations at www.flamewarriors.com, a website devoted to Internet insults. "To enter his Flame Warriors site is sort of like entering a hellish Sesame Street populated by Oscar the Grouch and 83 of his relatives." – Los Angeles Times.
(http://redwing.hutman.net/%7Emreed/warriorshtm/lat.htm)

Mike Reed has always enjoyed reading. As a young child, he liked the Dr. Seuss books. Later, he started reading biographies and war stories. One reason why he feels lucky to be an illustrator is because he can listen to books on tape while he works. Mike is available to provide custom illustrations for all manner of publications at reasonable prices. Mike can be reached at www.mikereedillustration.com.

Made in the USA
Charleston, SC
09 June 2014